the purpose of reality

lunar

steve simpson

Meerkat Press
Asheville

Cover art by Steve Simpson
llustrations by Steve Simpson
Book design by Tricia Reeks

Printed in the United States of America

Published in the United States of America by
Meerkat Press, LLC, Asheville, North Carolina
www.meerkatpress.com

To the memory of the Australian Poet Michael Dransfield (1948–1973), whose achievements in his tragically short life were a luminous inspiration.

Contents

Index of Illustrations

Simpson's visual evolution engine was used in the creation of the illustrations.

Anachrônia

Once the sun was planetary,
with the earth, its moon.
Once mornings began in auroral mysteries,
and gravity's rule was lighter than air.

Now the earth falls round the sun
and the moon around the earth,
but while our memories echo with violets
and fragrance, fragments of volition,
come with me, my friend.

Self-pity is a shoreline one
must not walk *a cappella.*
Come with me,
and we'll face our lives with living.

The tide of days never carried us,
its melody washes over us.
No sanctuary, no purity,
our shields and swords lie rusted
in the byways of the city's neon.

Yet every chance encounter
led us here, and on will lead us
in the final dance.

Through the night, a DJ's mellowed metal,
by the lyre, madrigals,
and in the sepia light of yesterdays,
we'll admire dewy cobwebs
on statues in a garden,
raise rattling breakfast cups
to those who've flown afar,
and do the crossword, two across:

    a crossroads
    a crossing
    to cross.

We've always known our ending waits
cretaceous on a chalky beach,
where the slate-gray skies
write white-horse lessons
on the blackboard sea—
the final class before our graduation.

But in these mortal moments,
when time is birdsong,
and the weather rests beneath a branch,
when distant evanescence hides in dreams,
come with me.

The Rest of Me

At the Café Économique,
they serve one class of patron,
one strength of resteamed coffee grounds,
a minor bird is hopping on a plastic olive branch,
and a mangy city cat is watching.

I'm seated at a graceless table
reading faded scrawls on a communal
paper napkin.

> *Some nights are filled with poison*
> *and the morning has no tourniquet,*
> *it seeps into the day.*
>
> *I gaze across the unforgiving sea*
> *at sunrise. My nets are in a tangle,*
> *and I sail in fishless circles.*
>
> *Some nights belong to the Marias—*
> *Maresia and Maré. They command*
> *the silvery fish to shine in spiral arms,*
> *to cluster in the corners of my cabin.*

I turn the napkin over.

So cold, their fallen light.
My schemes, my plans, my cravings
are Rorschach ink in their osmotic sky,
and yet they make the mornings honey sweet,
dress the winter sun in gaily colored knits,
in camouflaged ambivalence.

The rest has faded into coffee stains
and lipstick imprints, but angled in one corner,
two final words:

Goodbye, Renato[1]

~/~

In the square outside, the march of busyness
arrives, departs, commutes, in buses, taxis,
and machines that I don't recognize.

A wild wind is swelling, and grimy raindrops streak the café
windows.
Von Kármán vortex streets are trailing through the crowds,
that run or huddle or comment on the weather
—its unexpected forcefulness—
and one by one they're taken, swept aloft,
and gone.

~/~

Time passes, stays a while, I refill my coffee cup,
and notice there's a change outside:
while the groundlings rise and vanish in the clouds,
another group descends.

---

1. The intervening comma may exist, or may be the earthly
remains of a small insect.

A few land in the traffic and cause a snarl,
others come to the Économique
for coffee and a chat.

They cannot pay, they have no cash or cards
or clothes, but they open lines of credit.

A newcomer nods and seats herself nearby.
I make causal conversation
about our napkin and the weather,
about the curious cycle of events outside,
about living.

Could she possibly help me understand?

She does and I do.

She reconstructs the nightly sea:
its poisons and its sweets,
the fishing fleet and the two Marias,
Maresia and Maré,
the moon and her subservient stars.

Time's a two-way street,
I've reached the future,
the mysteries of the present
are all behind me now.

In a while, I'll notice the mobile phone
that's pressed against her ear,
and wonder if I'm merely listening in,
irrelevant in the shadows.

"Oh Renato," she'll say,
"I've given you the very best of me,"
and précis her farewell
in the corner of the napkin.

Sereia

Broadcast live from earth, ionic slivers inside skulls—
visions wired to words, stuttering, sparking, and Sereia.

She's painted the refrigerator red, the television too,
but at least it's just the screen.

click

The sound's a little damp, a little blue.
She must have done the audio as well.

A paint-smeared note reads

>   *Gone to buy more paint,*
>   *dinner's on the table.*

It's half-eaten spaghetti marinara take-out,
with half a glass of red, a little lipstick
on the rim, Bahia Sunset maybe.

~/~

"You must decide," Sereia told me,
"whether to seek the lighthouse,
or accept the ocean."

I've walked botanical avenues,
breathed the air chirped by sparrows,
and touched the quiet centerline of nothingness.

Yet there were always spectral shadows,
undiscovered secrets, unknown choices missed and gone,
other shades I never saw beyond each inflorescence,
all because I was searching for the lighthouse.

~/~

A car pulls up outside,
and a soldier crab scuttles
underneath the sofa.

Sereia has two shopping bags of cans and brushes.

"What do you think so far?" she asks.

Fish are darting round the coral walls,
the indoor weather blushes tropical red.

"I love what you've done with the place."

The Detective

I woke up slowly in an infinite plane,
and found I was a dried-out coffee stain
on the office floor.

By eight o'clock, I'd morphed into
a forgettable insect; in half an hour,
give or take, I was a kookaburra
pecking at the floorboards,
and when a customer knocked at nine,
I was vaguely human, vaguely a detective,
polite, denatured, and unnatural.

Horizontal Departure

My client was dressed in gray-scale
with retrolescent highlights,
hand-tinted, frame by frame.

She asked if I was qualified to solve
her case, and when I pointed out my prized
achievement, she was unimpressed.

"This is a diploma in designing
counterfeit certificates,

awarded *magna cum laude*."

I had ready explanations.

"It depends on who reads it.
The quantum onlooker always changes
what's onlooked. And it was left here
by the previous occupant,
an investment adviser, as I recall."

She galloped her impatient fingertips
on my packing-crate desk.

"Let's get down to business, shall we?
When we study, when we learn,
Jakaíra, the goddess of the clouds,
takes away our fantasies. They vanish
like morning mist in sunlight.

"When I mastered quantum mechanics,
an important dream was lost.
I need to rediscover what lies beyond
the obsidian ocean."

"Your case is curiously nonsensical,
but I'm not the kind of detective
who rushes headlong into anything at all.
My decisions are based on logic and reason,
and what my horoscope says."

I studied my diary, scratchings on the wall—
shaky rows of four with diagonal reinforcement.

"With Aquarius ascendant, I have
a little brooding and moping,
with hand-wringing, if time permits,

on my schedule for today,
but I think that I can fit you in."

My client suggested casual stimulation.

"We could discuss the obsidian ocean
at the Café Économique.
Partially ground coffee's on special,
and it's just across the street."

"I'm afraid I cannot go with you."

Before my revelation, I undertook
a brief but suspenseful study of my nails.

"I'm imprisoned in this office,
and I can never leave."

"Well I came in, didn't I?"

"You quantum teleported
and knocked once you were inside."

I didn't call myself a detective for nothing.

She shrugged.

"Then how will you resolve my case?"

"A single phone call should be sufficient.
I'll contact Black Sea Tourist Information."

My client tapped a foot and paced,
fished in her Gucci handbag, and retrieved
an origami model of a crumpled piece of paper,
a Smith & Wesson .38,

and a fish, as logic dictated.

She targeted my crescent-moon glasses
with the fish, and by unexpected salmon magic,
doors appeared in the walls, the floor, and the ceiling.

After a brief discussion, counterpoint,
and rapprochement, we chose to depart
in a horizontal and westerly direction.

Apocalyptic Mozart

"The sunlight hurts my eyes.
I'm unaccustomed to the lack of walls,
and I miss the certainties
my office prison provided me."

My client used a spray can
to tint my glasses desert rose,
and thoughtfully plastered zinc cream
on my nose, but the world was not
as I expected.

Around me, tidy squares of rubble stretched
into the distance, to where the Sydney
skyline used to be.

It had been replaced by swirls of gritty smoke
rising to serrated cilia in the maws
of giant clam shells, spinning up above.

I heard the westerly wind carrying
Köchel 626 in gentle swell and fade,
and turned to my client, my eyebrows
asking a musical question.

"Oh, sorry, I forgot to mention. The planet's been

invaded by the bivalves, mineralized alien life
that dines on concrete and brickwork.
They dissolve it with acidic emissions.
By good fortune, structures like your office,
made of packing crates, don't interest them."

I decided a mild rebuke was called for.

"Such details might appear insignificant,
but they could be vital to the case.
Is there anything else you'd like to share?"

She offered me a breath mint.

"Their vaporous emissions are deadly
to flowers and fauns, and to humans.
I'm not sure anyone's survived,
apart from you and I."

I nodded. "Good to know, good to know."

She looked me up and down.

"I'm not the only one with secrets, am I?"

I felt my nose and cheeks,
they were embarrassingly furry.
Most of me was.

"RMD. It's genetic, and it's more common
than you might think. I mostly morph at night."

"What do the initials stand for?"

I mumbled my reply, trying to keep
my mouth closed. The teeth inside
felt rather sharp.

"The doctor never told me."

HOUSEHOLD WASTE

We wandered through the fractured
cityscape, searching for my client's dream,
a fantasy from long ago.

At dusk, we reached a tidy hamlet,
where all the fallen houses
were numbered zero.

Humanity was gone, but an urban planner's
wet scheme was left behind: roundabouts
and cul-de-sacs, and a pocket park
with deserted swings and slippery dips.

Was this my client's childhood archipelago
before the devastation, where the season
was always spring, and every day was dusted
with the future's sparking mysteries?

I asked, and she nodded.

I was pleased with my second detecting
success, and I wondered whether it was time
to mention that she was my first client,
and I had yet to solve a single case.

But only for a passing moment.

She took in the surroundings,
with sorrow at the edges of her eyes.

"Yes, this is where I spent my childhood,

where all dreams begin. A bubble
of forgotten memory may rise to the surface
of my thoughts, or you might find a clue."

She sighed.

"To the dearest strangers of our blood,
we become no more than symbols,
with our personal realities inaccessible beneath."

Our mutual silence was unmuted
by a heap of refuse on the sidewalk.

"Might I join you in your travels?
I have a broad curriculum vitae,
I've worked in various capacities,
and I'm currently available for an interview."

Even apocalyptic fantasy has its limits.

"I'm not ungrateful for your offer,
but I'm afraid that, although
I take the garbage out on occasion,
I rarely keep its company."

Flashing pinpoint lights illuminated the mound.

"Humans, all the same,
they see a little trash
and decide to add their own."

I looked more closely. Beneath the rusted
all-in-one utensils, the empty bottles
and fast-food wrappers, the remaindered
stockings and sneakers—transient memento mori—

there was a buzz and a glow, a knot
of jumbled wires and a flickering
of krytron valves.

"My name is Cyber Think
and I know more than any iPhone.
My rationality, my literality,
is the burden I must bear,
yet all I am to humans is a means
to hide their own illogic.

"For you, the greatest beauty
will always be a mystery:
neither simple Turing machines,
Fermat's last conjecture . . .
woof bark . . . bark woof . . ."

I'd lost interest in his monotonous monologue.

"That's enough," my client said,
and targeted him with her used-to-be fish,
which had unexpectedly become
an axolotl, grasping an even smaller
axolotl in its primitive hand.

"I beg you, let me come along,
I won't hold you back. Although
I have no obvious means
of locomotion, I will find a way."

My client responded with unexpected kindness.

"You may join us if you meet
the entrance requirement.
You must answer a question
taught me by the Sphinx of Thebes:

'On our journey, what's the chance
that anything at all will make
some kind of sense?'"

With flashes, sparks, and sizzling,
black smoke billowing, Cyber Think replied.

"You have asked a circular question,
entirely dependent on itself.

"This world must already be rational,
and make sense, for chance and probability
to be calculated. Like Microsoft Excel,
I've recovered from the circularity.

"My answer is logically complete,
let us be on our way."

And Cyber Think achieved a curious featherless flight
through mind alone,
becoming an improbable
inverse phoenix
that ascended,
burning ardently,
and dissipated to a cloud of ash and greasy smoke.

In the light of the setting sun,
filtered through the dust
of pulverized human habitation
left by the bivalves, the visual
was spectacular.

SAFE WAYS

We journeyed on toward a hidden horizon,
where the distant bivalves were silvery phantoms,

photoluminescent contradictions in the darkness.

My client had her axolotl armaments,
and I might have been brave,
but I was a frightened woodland creature
seeking refuge from the restless night.

Metaphorically. Metaphorically,
a frightened woodland creature.

She made a stop sign with her hand,
although it wasn't hexagonal.

"Over there, a building is still standing.
We'll rest until the daylight."

~/~

When I awoke from a dream of death,
I found that I was the usual coffee stain,
and after a transformative sequence,
I was close enough to a human
doing the shopping without a cart,
surrounded by packs of batteries,
pegs, and colorful party favors.

Further down the aisle, where the shelves
were penned and papered, an old man,
no different to any other, was atoning
for his sins by writing penitential pages
of schoolboy repetitions.

The time had come for me to be
the detective I was meant to be,
and I attended closely to my surroundings.

In the following aisle, person A,
named with an initial initial,
was sorting all the gaudy product on the shelves,
arranging like with like: disinfectants
and detergents, air fresheners and floor polish,
interspersed with pine cones, lemons,
and sprigs of lavender.

A yellow warning sign read,
Surrealism when wet.

Next across, persons B and C
were combing, brushing, and spraying on
a range of promised miracles,
or their money back.

The denizens of the pet food aisle
had no interest in chemical fantasies
or bacterial annihilation.
Cat D was snoozing, while cockatoos E to R
were pecking at the packages of seed,
the shelving, and supporting structures.

Still further on, amongst the fizzy drinks,
I found homologous axolotls X and x
guzzling Fanta through straws with stripes.

My head was filled with clues.
It was time to add a dash of logic,
a twist of mystery, and top it off
with random guesswork.

All of us were shipwreck survivors,
together and alone, the desolate remainder
of a division we never understood,

and in the parking lot, my client's sea
was roiling darkness.

Her dream, her missing fantasy,
was prescient, an omen now become
intransigent reality, and beyond her ocean,
the bivalves were inevitable.

And yet, I had some doubts.
What were the roles of the cockatoos,
the cat, and penguins S to W,
whom I forgot to mention?

While I was puzzling, I remembered that
I'd heard my client calling out to me:
We have to get away from here.

But without an exclamation point,
I hadn't paid attention, even though
the axolotls had scurried off to join her.

A sudden rush of sound disturbed
my mental merry-go-round.

The ceiling and the roof dissolved,
breakfast for a bivalve, and a curling snake
of sulfurous vapor scorched my eyes,
ran bitter in my nose and throat,
like the small red chilies one should
never purchase.

The Reliability of Expectations 1

It was unprofessional in every way.

When I scuttled out of the rubble,

the axolotls and the penguins
kept their distance.

I might have been an acid-resistant
prehistoric lizard, but I certainly
wasn't carnivorous.

My client petted me, tickled
my wattled chin, and I felt my scales
glowing.

~/~

"Would you mind looking after my diary?"

She examined the constellations of stars
and crescent moons on my boxer shorts.

"They were all I could find. And the diary
has my notes on the case. For safekeeping,
in case there's another . . . inconvenience."

THE RELIABILITY OF EXPECTATIONS 2

It was no one's fault, not his nor mine,
and even the bivalves weren't to blame.

How they came to be, their nature,
their perception of the world,
all of it lies beyond our understanding,
but they're living creatures, borne below
and risen from deep within the earth.

What we see as willed destruction
is only of their bivalve nature,
without morality, or cognizance

of right and wrong.

~/~

It happened on Parramatta's outskirts,
where we'd stopped for tea and bickies.

In the remnants of a Five and a Half - Seven,
the detective had sought out mineral water,
sparkling at a pinch, for the axolotls and penguins.

A ravenous bivalve appeared above the bowsers,
its exothermic acid reacted with the alkaline concrete,
gasoline leaking from an underground tank caught fire,
and before his chameleonics could save him,
he was consumed in the fireball.

We held a simple ceremony beneath the falling ash.
Penguin T in somber black and white cheeped
a requiem in Latin, and I wiped my eyes
and blew my nose, whispered my name
for his ghost to know.

THE GOLDEN PENGUIN'S TIMETABLE

We crossed the mountains single file,
through the scratchy bushland,
and to the mocking calls of kookaburras,
we left the urban ruination far behind.

Now our pilgrimage continues,
in the cool of morning,
when the golden penguin goddess
awakens from her snowy dreams,
and through the evenings, when she waddles

to her nest beneath the world.[1]

Out into the western distance,
where the heat haze merges
with the mistakable horizon,
I've seen sparks and flashes,
glimmers of expectation,
day by day growing clearer.

The age of modular concrete,
of modulated inconvenience,
is in the past, obliterated,
and magic is incipient.

Somewhere on the westward plains,
our struggles will be new ones,
and I'll recall a touch of truth
that I once knew.

REALITY AND CYCLICITY

I journey onward to the west,
with my coterie of penguins
and axolotls.

We discover country corners,
where strangers make believe
their ordinary lives have not been lost:
motels with sewing kits
and swimming pools for guests,
where the penguins jump and splash,
dance their stately dances,
raise their beaks to the stars,

---

1. Penguins believe the earth is flat.

with enthusiastic cries of 'encore'
from the axolotls.

The outline of our destination is unmistakable now,
with slender spires
and glass-blown towers, improbable cathedrals
that refract the slanting light
prismatically, proposing beauty over function.

The City is a beachhead from another plane,
but it's impermanent.
Like thoughts awakening, still half-formed,
that evaporate too soon,
it follows a diurnal cycle with sunlit synchronicity.

By the turn of evening, it's riddled with a net of fractures,
a mirage of sparking
crystal fragments fading. And with the light of every dawn
comes coalescence,
its facets reconstruct themselves, reassert their multistoried
reality.

The arc of its existence is not assured by
dowdy human solidity.
It has no skeletal enforcement, no shell without
nor blueprint within.

In the timorous recesses of my mind,
I fear that, in its self-annihilation,
the City is refuting itself.

Its alien gods are not yet satisfied,
and its day-to-day unmaking leaves me
restless.

~/~

Last night I dreamed with the detective.

He looked up from his basalt desk and smiled,
inquired after the penguins and the axolotls.

"All are in good spirits," I replied,
"I'm teaching the axolotls quantum
mechanics for beginners,"
and asked a question of my own,
with a sprinkling of flattery.

"Your notebook was less than useless,
but you know more than any living soul,
you've reached the furthest shoreline
of the obsidian ocean.

"So tell me, will the Crystal City
offer sanctuary from the bivalves?
Is that place the answer to my quest?"

The detective studied his fingernails,
and shrugged.

"Your ignorance is limitless.
What you don't know stretches beyond
Wallerawang, beyond Perth. A little more
hardly seems to matter."

He was more arrogant in death.

"You made a promise, and my generous
deposit will never be refunded."

"Well, I suppose . . . woof bark . . . bark woof."

The detective had abruptly morphed into

a small yapping poodle.

After a moment, he reappeared, chastened.

"I apologize. I still have RMD in this place,
although I know what the initials stand for now.
My body has a mind of its own,
and it punishes me whenever it sees fit.

"And I've learned that I was not born a human."

He sighed.

"The Crystal City is home to the unearthly.
It's not your destination.

"If you divert around it, you'll soon arrive at
New Wallerawang, a town of packing crates
and shipping containers, impressively constructed
to several stories, with wooden ladders
and zig-zag walkways.

"Human ingenuity at its finest,
and the Five and a Half – Seven there
has a special on sparkling water."

~/~

Thinking back in the woken light of day,
I've come to realize that childhood fantasies
are childhood fantasies, no more and no less,
and I'm not meant to be anything
other than truly human.

And with the lessons his body
teaches him, I'm certain the detective

will reinvent himself, become
the very best that he may be.

For now, New Wallerawang is waiting.

The Return of Doctor Petal

"Before lunch, I'll distill the embrocation of the morning
from sunrise animalia, from human sweetness,
and capture the morphic essence of the caterpillar
and the cicada."

Breakfast with the inestimable Doctor Petal,
who mentioned on Instagram that she'd come
to earth to study what was falling in the rain,
to tidy things up a bit—a little urban annihilation
with her antimatter laser—and because a spare planet
was always handy.

My self-esteem replies.

"Would like a piece of me?"

"There are plenty of caterpillars in the garden."

~/~

At lunch, I try for enigmatic and unpredictable,
flap my arms a little, and speak of the arctic aardvark.

"You have no secrets, earthling.

"Farewells ride on all your stories,
spur them on when your mind
is burning to your fingertips,
when your heart is in the freezer
beneath the frozen peas
that you purchased in 1969."

~/~

After dinner, Doctor Petal goes to the graveyard
to study human history. She runs her fingers
over chiseled headstones, and whispers chosen names.

They all start out as knots of air, tightly coiled,
but soon enough, they're chatting about their lives,
one hundred years ago.

Once she hinted that she'd called me back as well.

But even though I might have been emulsified
and reticulated by the good doctor, and on rainy days,
I see a figurine of speech reflected in the mirror,
I'm as real as I might be.

My early memories flash with shining astral bodies,
and my path is guided by electric fireflies.

And no one, not even the remarkable Doctor Petal,
    can tell me
    what is taken,
    what is given,
    or what's transformed,
on the bridge that crosses the river of transcendence.

The Egg in White

I was once a nervous invitee
at an exponential function
hosted by his eminence,
the summit of his self-creation;
close acquaintances only, commonality
reassured in glyphic communication.

His hacienda was mostly atria,
potted green, with rain-washed
marble chessboards, where gardeners
wearing chefs' hats offered fertilizer
and entrées.

"Memories, if compressed by force,
achieve solidity, quite attractive
although immobilized," he told me,
and took me on a tour.

~/~

Beneath a shade-cloth willow,
a selected group debated lies and fantasy,
with imported whiskey, ice, and me,
wound in a Roman bedsheet,
a little anxious in such brightly illustrated
company.

At a certain unremarkable moment,
his eminence leaned toward me, *sotto voce*:

"The magic of my youth has left me,
its cicadas and ephemeral smoke.

"Once I fell in love with a vagrant light,
a luminous firefly, and now I seek a book
she wrote, about verity, magic, and myrrh—
'The Egg in White.'

"Might you help me in my quest?"

I feigned a degree of contemplation,
looked up into the windy sky,
where a storm of truth was brewing,
and dissembled with a flourish of my glass.

"An Isley single malt if I'm not mistaken.
Do you mean magic magic or just plain magic?
Might this egg have been instead, a pale amber shade,
and within, the ashes of a phoenix?
And which came first, the book or the egg?"

After sunset, I observed the other guests—
they didn't leave, they found their places
in the corridors, or on the plinths in alcoves.
Each returned to a static life, each no more
than a cobwebbed recollection of his eminence.

When We're Real

"It's time for me to go."

"Haven't you seen the news?
The Venusians are invading.
They've been studying us for years,
collecting all our confidential thoughts.
Their conquest of the earth is underway.
You're safer in the coffee shop with me."

Estrelinha sighed.

"Alright then, tell me more.
The Twitter version please."

"Their spacecraft are powered by stellarators
and imitation science. They locomote
on tentacles in a starfish arrangement,
and they wear fluorescent makeup.

"But their spies are cloaked in optical illusions
and stroboscopic deflections, just like humans.
Underneath, they're galaxies in glass,
spiral arms and silver watercolors,
diamond flames from time's beginning.

"I've seen them gliding down the highways

"

in Toyota Starlets, two-tone, blue and gray,
and they're occupying mountain tops
and Starbucks, planning global terraforms
and media hallucinants—
two hundred football channels,
Huxley one, Orwell zero."

Estrelinha was unconvinced. She looked outside,
at the evening's pedestrians.

"Everything's normal enough out there.
Someone's accosting strangers,
and warning them of something.
They're on a pogo stick,
and they look like you,
apart from the wig."

Did she mean I had a wig,
or was it the pogo person?
I decided not to ask.

"The astute are watching
Netflix in secure basements,
silicone sealed against Venusians.
I've done a bit myself."

She sighed more convincingly.

"You and I were never miscible:
balsamic vinegar and oil."

"A garden salad, a blueberry muffin,
another coffee perhaps? All the famous cats
are on Instagram, but I am here."

"My life is waiting beyond your gravity well,"
and she called to the waiter.

Goodbye was written across her forehead.
I had nothing to lose, and I chose to babble.

"I've made measurements in vacuo,
dropped a bottle and a feather:
the bottle floated through the window,
the feather weighed upon my thoughts.

"Streets and streetlamps, starfish in the square,
silent letters and raucous seagulls.
Do they serve a purpose?

"What's the use of poetry and pogo sticks?
Of crystal beaches, Beowulf in winter socks,
the blue electric?

"When I'm with you, I wonder."

"Every time you open your mouth,
reality plays with her phone."

But Estrelinha was still with me at the table.

"We're only real when we're
unwritten, unrecorded."

The Perfidy of Memory

Three café explorations.

Reading Choices

"Reality serves at memory's pleasure,
something I read somewhere."

"I have a tattoo with the very same words."

"Quite the coincidence."

"I'm whimsically curious
about your reading choices,
about the when and where."

"Details I've forgotten,
I'm afraid. I wasn't paying
close attention."

Thanks for the Memory

She offered me the pack of Marlboro Memories.
I accepted, and I'd finished one a moment before,
a fade of smoke, an echoed warmth

congealed against my throat.

I squinted at the blackboard menu,
chalked, rechalked, patchworked
with erasures, crossings out.

"I'll have a latte, Abstinence Three's on special.
First sip is three-day retrograde deletion
of memories of caffeine. Peak craving, so they say."

"How's the bird repair shop going?"

"As slowly as an infinite regress:
leak repairs for a scuba-diving cormorant,
an orthonormalizing engine for an interstellar sparrow,
and for a boa, feather implants."

When I asked about her notes,
she turned the page through space and time
from twelve to three o'clock.

"What's been redacted?"

"Your second coffee erased
your recollection of the first."

"Did someone say, *We're made of memories*?"

"Deleted from your personal timeline,
along with coffee number one."

MAGIC AND THE NIGHT

She leaned across the table
in a cloud of scented whispers.

"It's the latest in synaptic fashion:

customized forgetting.
I'll be erased from you,
a month of us together gone,
and when we meet tomorrow,
it will be a celebration.

"Magic and the Night,
at the Transcendent Trattoria,
with cacciatore free-range chicken,
liberated from their earthly cages.

"*Querido*, if you love me,
won't you please forget me?"

He sipped his old-fashioned coffee.

"Every moment is a token we've created,
coffee instants, you and me
in post-it note reminders.
We're made of what we make ourselves
in pendant circularity,
spirals paired and interwoven.

"So no, *amor*, I won't."

Requiem for the Toaster

In the west, two rivers merge,
the flows of past and future
mingle with the guests,
a meet and greet.

From the shore, in a certain quality of light,
you may glimpse a flight in gray,
a moving blueprint, a system of soft levers.

Ciphers, written on the foliage
in efflorescent mimicry,
will come and go to seed,
and you may touch a lesser happiness
before the wheel of ending
makes a single turn.

We're streaky light in morning darkness,
if not that, then something else,
defined by artifice and circumstance,
woven in a stranger's scarf, Italian knit.

"What's that?"

"My requiem for the toaster."

"Is it under warranty? You should take it back."

Shared Laundry Rules

1. Do not eat the soap,
    or suggest the same
    to an acquaintance.

2. Do not penultimately decide
    that you will wash a household pet
    or your current outfit, in situ.

3. Check all pockets for relevant receipts,
    including toaster purchases,
    even if you're wondering
    who left the scarf in the machine,
    and whether they used the delicate cycle.

    Or if, when it is half past two,
    why the soap is half past two,
    why your clothes are half past two,
    and why the stranger's scarf is half past two.

"The docket went through the wash,
and when I pegged it on the line,
a crow flew down and pecked it off,
took it to feed her young."

My counterpoint on keyboard played
a dark accompaniment,
a little *capriccioso, ma non troppo,*
and I confessed a peccadillo or two.

"I had a breakfast craving,
an impatience for some high-speed toast.
I put the toaster in the microwave,
and the microwave on the stove.

"I have several requiems to write."

Homo Sapiens,
Beta Release

This is the tale of Proteus,
the legendary beta man,
the greatest and only scientist of the Jurassic,
friend to the tasteless simpsonodon[1]
and the slightly feathered archaeopteryx,
as bearded as da Vinci, and in whose hair,
a flickering of iridescent wings,
mostly still attached to dragonflies,
glittered in the sunlight.

Proteus, who discovered fire and put it out,
who invented a sinuous and somewhat snakely
dance he liked to call the mambo,
who assembled wheels and axles
to create a rudimentary encyclopedia
that he pedaled across Gondwanaland
on weekends, determined with a sundial
to be whenever he saw fit.

––––––––––––

1. The simpsonodon was a small Jurassic mammal named after
the noted paleontologist G.G. Simpson.

When silent luminosity muted calls
of unseen creatures in the synesthetic night,
and sleep played hide-and-seek,
Proteus scratched his prescient ears
and speculated on his future.

He saw that he would rest in layered shale,
interleaved and carboniferous,
until his earthly particles evanesced
above an ancient tar pit: a morning mist
in the era of the plasticine Anthropocene.

He was all alone, all and only of himself,
and though he might have carved a sigil
here and there, in the trunk of a giant fern,
or in the southern regions of a dozing diplodocus,
and he took a certain pride in his recipe
for simpsonodon à la mode,
he knew he was no Ozymandias,
and soon enough, he'd be forgotten.

~/~

And yet, thanks to dandelion puffballs,
and their lack of any connection with
multi-syllabic paleoanthropological hoaxes,
the highlights of the life of Proteus
have been unexpectedly recovered from my rubbish bin,
where they lay hidden beneath assorted empty bottles.

A Wistful Lament

As it happened, Proteus couldn't speak with sounds:
when he opened his mouth and set his throat to vibrate,
glowing bubbles, leafy baubles, necklaced seeds

—a myriad of elemental protozoan shapes—
floated from his lips, sparkling and drifting through the trees.

My return, he thought, *the balance of me,*
being made from nothing, to which I must revert.

I cannot sing the sweet love calls
of the gentle diplodocus, nor, like the pterodactyl,
screech to my compadres to scatter timid herds of mammals,
and the wistful lament of a soliloquy will never cross my lips.
But I have no use for such pretense,
my solitude is my strength.

Momentarily, Proteus changed his mind.

~/~

In a pool of faded lunar light,
he found a tiny mummified body.

He cupped it in his hand and addressed it
with cascading firefly points, interleaved
with glow-worm dashes, a little like Morse Code.

> *Oh curious creature, I shall name you, 'Yorick.'*
> *Your tail was long but your life was short,*
> *and your genus and species are a mystery*
> *that humans may never solve.*
>
> *Like you, I have lived my life tenuously,*
> *unable to ascertain who I am*
> *or where I'm going.*
>
> *I will wear your body on a necklace*
> *against my heart, as soon as I determine*

precisely where that is,
and I'll travel far and wide,
peddling across Gondwanaland,
until I find a place where your
delicate bones may be preserved,
and some monocled paleontologist
will unearth them in the distant future.

In that way, I'll ensure
the recognition of your kind.

But the chameleon-like creature,
whose skin resembled powdery dust,
had merely been napping.

It awoke abruptly, nipped off a sample
of Proteus' little finger, scurried along his arm,
and fled.

A Lighthouse By Any Other Name

If only I could speak,
engage in conversation
with anyone at all,
I'd be sage and silent.

Archie, the archaeopteryx
whom Proteus addressed,
ignored the paper lantern lights
floating from his mouth.

I wouldn't babble, spout
immaterial lunar permutations
concerning plausible fish,
or the iridescent creature

I recently remarked on the headland
by the iron-sand beach.

All in a dream, a stranger told me
it's better not to relate your dreams,
because no one ever cares, although
they may feign interest, and in the exception
which proved the rule, he mentioned that,
in his own dreams, a doppelgänger
from the primeval void follows him
everywhere he goes.

But come to think of it,
what was that luminous lifeform?

It shone so brightly by the sea,
like a tall, cylindrical house
with a light inside.

~/~

Proteus returned to the headland,
with Archie perched upon his head,
and sought out the glowing being,
who was taking a stroll, an evening
constitutional, beside the sea.

Archie swooped around the stranger,
no doubt hoping he could snip a tasty moth
attracted by the light, and Proteus shyly
emitted a little visual conversation.

I hear the tygers will be burning
symmetrically
in the jungle tonight.

"An anachronism. William Blake,

if I'm not mistaken."

Proteus was astounded.
The creature had understood him,
and replied acoustically.

Vanitas

The stranger introduced herself to Proteus.

"I've named myself Evita,
and you're the conduit of my creation.
Not your ribs, but your intangible phrases
that weave the darkness
with their phosphorescent trails.

"Out over the ocean,
between the near and far,
they reconnected, coalesced,
and here I am."

Proteus was quintessentially humble,
but because he couldn't count
as high as quintessential,
and because he thought that he alone
had created the glorious Evita,
he chose to elaborate
his personal achievements.

> *. . . the fish were simply flapping there,*
> *although one was slightly nibbled on the tail,*
> *and I deduced that they were four*
> *in number . . .*

> *. . . and not a trilobite in the pool,*
> *because they became extinct*
> *at the end of the Paleozoic,*

so finally, I could count from zero
all the way to four . . .

. . . the diplodocuses charged,
and as I fled between the cycads,
I enumerated their legs:
an indeterminate number,
and dividing by four,
I ascertained the object-oriented tally,
another indeterminate number.
I call this 'computing.'

Evita professed an unexpected interest
in the natural numbers.

"*Fascinante*. Please,
tell me more about two."

Proteus was mesmerized
by the glitter of his own words,
reflected in Evita's eyes.

On he went, sprinkling
his numerical ascent in powers of two
with exaggerations,
and he paid scant attention when Archie
undertook urgent
aeronautical acrobatics nearby.

He didn't know, and neither did I,
that the pseudo-bird
was trying to warn him of an imminent
inconvenience.

MORNING LIGHTS

When the morning's sun had filled

the shadows of the moon,
Proteus had an inkling that his feeble wisdom
didn't limit the world, and recognized
the twin subversions of his vanity
—ignorance and arrogance—
but the revelations came too late.

"Hold on a sec."

Evita turned away,
and Proteus followed her gaze.

A newly formed creation was approaching
along the beach, an unexpected byproduct of
the boastful torrent of protozoa that Proteus
had emitted.

Evita, Número Uno, admired Número Dos.

"Oh, such delectable burning symmetry.
I have rhetorical questions concerning
proton fusion in the cores of stars, and you."

"Cool. I call myself Adamstown."

Número Dos was stripier than Evita,
but he certainly wasn't stellar in any way.
That's what Proteus told himself.

Evita and Adamstown looked to the sunrise,
looked to the western horizon,
and Evita turned to Proteus,
who was trying to count his toes.

"I will hold you in my core,

where cooler fusion powers me.
You enabled my existence."

Adamstown was more succinct.

"Ditto, dude. Later."

Their ionized auras flared, joined,
and they were gone, from the land to the ocean,
skimming low, with the foaming waves
arching, reaching upward to touch them.

Proteus uttered a series of exclamation points,
and the nimble archaeopteryx narrowly avoided
a blowtorch defeathering.

Boldly Knitting

The devastated Proteus moped
in the Jurassic jungle, nights fell
and days broke, until, at last,
a random thought appeared,
somewhere in his beard.

> *By my words alone, I will generate*
> *the necessities of modern life.*
>
> *Behold, when I say, 'lightbulb,'*
>
> *lightbulb*
>
> *a lightbulb appears.*

The shapes that sprang from his mouth
were not unlike unsuccessful balloon twistings

of micro-sized baboons, but Proteus was pleased,
having no idea what a lightbulb might be.

Archie, who enabled the soliloquy,
thought that the curious entities
looked rather tasty. He snaffled them up,
and swallowed them.

After his success with domestic lighting,
Proteus couldn't help but think about Evita,
the charming plasmoid who'd inverted
all his dreams.

> *Although she's far away, I will find her,*
> *and bring her back to me.*
>
> *Adamstown, who took her from me,*
> *is striped from his head to his (possibly*
> *metaphorical) tail, so I will boldly*
> *knit myself a comparable sweater*
> *with matching scarf and beanie.*
> *And since the weather's turning chilly,*
> *I'll fashion it from wool.*
>
> *But first off, I'll need sheep.*

When Proteus said 'sheep,' he exhaled
a fluorescent filament that wove the air.

He was unsure of a sufficiency of 'sheep,'
and, in any case, he could only count to four—
five glowing threads in his Jurassic version
of the C Programming Language,
which includes zero.

On and on he went, until,
not unexpectedly, he fell asleep,

and he continued in his dreams,
murmuring their name.

RETURN TO THE BEACH

Proteus was awoken by nocturnal rustles,
roars, and yawns, but not a single bleat.

We must return to the iron-sand beach,
he advised his mute and mildly feathered companion,
and with surprising perspicacity, he added,
that is where the magnetite confines
my luminous emanations, and the creatures
are drawn there.

~/~

Proteus arrived in time to see the final sheep departing,
the incandescent stragglers of the flock—
the Arietids rising, dwindling to starry points
on their journey to Aries, the woolen constellation.

"Do you think you might say 'lightbulb' again?"
Archie asked, "I'm feeling a little peckish."

~/~

His mouth was gaping open,
evincing carefree dental hygiene,
but Proteus was speechless,
in a manner of speaking.

Archie might have been an ancient bird,
but he was no Jurassic fool.

"We have to be logical, my friend.
Now that your creative light's inside me,

I speak with sounds, like Adamstown
and Evita.

"And you can be with her again,
your beloved Evita,
the incompatible lifeform
you recently met.

"But before I tell you how,
we must come to an arrangement."

Mutual Recursion

"Evita is shockingly electric,
and would stop your heart
at the slightest touch,
but there's a way to safely seek
her company."

    Lightbulb, lightbulb.

Proteus spoke according to his agreement
with Archie, who snuffled up each luminous
entrée created by that word.

    And what is that way?
    Lightbulb, lightbulb.

"You must create a radiant clone.
You must speak your lonely name,
and your transcendental echo
will walk hand-in-hand with Evita."

While Proteus prevaricated, I decided
it would be inconvenient to record
further mentions of lightbulbs.

That other me . . . will not be me,
. . . or if it's me . . . I won't be.

The ancient bird shrugged, implausibly.

"Let's not get metaphysical.
Something we have never known
we cannot long for.
It's the best that you can do."

Proteus agreed, and began the recitation
of his name.

~/~

Proteus II, the new luminous plasmoid version,
shook his head, and replied with his sounds.

"Get real, dude, this is the modern Jurassic.
I won't be skipping across the ocean like a song,
chasing some enigmatic stranger.
The salt water might short-circuit
my internal fluxes."

The two versions of Proteus debated,
contradictory light and sound,
until Archie interceded.

"Look."

The words of Proteus II had produced
their own creations: solid protozoan shapes
that crawled and wriggled on the iron sand.

The Proteus duo agreed on the insignificance
of the observation, equally incorrectly.

"So what?"

    Who cares?

"Don't you see, you prehistoric buffoons?
If Proteus II repeats the name 'Evita,'
she'll coalesce in flesh and fluid form."

MODESTY

When Evita of the earth arrived,
Proteus didn't expound
his theory of countability:
he'd somewhat learned a lesson.

Instead, he showed her his encyclopedia,
being wary not to speak too much.

Evita studied Proteus thoughtfully,
paying close attention to the denizens of his beard,
and afterward, prepared a shopping list
for Proteus II, who agreed to recite it.

". . . an all-cotton jumpsuit, medium size,
with a Mondrian print; extra-large overalls;
a cut-throat razor; breath freshener . . ."

~/~

Proteus II was impressed with his bleeding beardless other.

"Cool, dude. Who would have guessed
what was hiding underneath?"

He sighed.

"You're know you're like a brother to me,

but there's something I must tell you.
You're not the archetype, not the original,
not at all. You're not the first of us.

"In a dreamless time before this time of dreams,
I said, 'Dude,' and you appeared:
solids, liquids, and quite a bit of gas."

Proteus was unimpressed, and the brothers
took to arguing over who was the chook
and who was the egg, with numerous examples
materializing.

Diversity

With questions of Jurassic fashion resolved,
Evita found a sapling and whipped them both
around their heads.

> *Behave yourselves,*
> *you see no further than each other,*
> *yet your vanity knows no bounds.*

The brothers Proteus paid no heed,
but in the end, with glowing ears
(literal and not), they realized that
their circular arguing was tiresome,
and childish.

"I have plans," Proteus II announced,
"I'll be traveling to the future Ethiopia.[2]
The prototyping phase is over,
it's time for the production version."

---

2. Proteus II took over 100 million years to arrive, so he must
have dawdled.

Proteus felt the need to match his brother.

> If it's foretold by the woolly stars tonight,
> I may invent decaffeinated coffee,
> or otherwise, conditional phrases
> are on the cards.

Evita was decisive.

> Too *much* does not exist, too little does.
> We'll ride the skyward winds on pterosaurs,
> cross the mountains to an evergreen plain:
> a checkerboard of orchards, with Granny Smiths
> and a snake or two.

> There, *we* will see what may be called
> into existence.

Archie, the demure archaeopteryx,
took an interest.

"Snakes? Rather tasty I expect."

When will the mowing be done?

The motor stutters and misses,
the blades strike sparks off stones.
He mows the lawn to dullness and straw
while he dreams of crystal forests,
of garden glades, and Gaia.

In the tunnel of the last afternoon,
when the angels of air fall burning to earth,
and the angels of rain are lost at sea,
the mowers will rust in the meadows of ash
and no one will need to mow.

Solar Disenchantment

In the early hours, I was lost in demi-dreams.
I couldn't find the sun beneath my pillow,
but I met the windwalkers, who whispered
in the megahertz range, with occasional
interjections from summer's lightbulb lightning.

The windwalkers informed me
that the sun had been carefully packaged
in environmentally friendly
chromospheric wrapping,
but someone had misread
the intergalactic address—
a three much like an eight.

Now it was en route again,
with a *Return to Sender* sticker.

~/~

When the sun finally turned up,
it was high above the horizon,
and I was up there too, still sleeping,
searching for the sky's blue caves,
like I always do.

The light of day was shining in
through the bedroom window,
and waking up was only a moment away.

I pulled the ripcord and my parachute opened.
I descended gently, though the air was thin
and atmospheric heartbeats
were rushing in my ears.

~/~

"Same old dream,
oversimplifying everything,
never passing through
the surfaces of time."

That was Deija, the Princess of Glass,
and well-known Martian know-it-all.

I apologized insincerely.

Longitude Étude

I chose a seat at the back of the forever bus,
while Deija drove down longitudes,
across deficits of land and surpluses of sea,
navigated corridors of power grids,
to where botanical bones were burning
in equatorial flames.

~/~

We reached the polar southern land
too late, the ice floes had already
turned to ice water, and the ultraviolets

had blossomed long before
on the panascopic shores.

"What will we do now?" I asked.

"We'll do what people do in rowboats."

I searched for oars,
and Deija mixed gin tonics.

~/~

It was early or late, and I'd drifted
to low tide in the gin bottle.

"The windwalkers told me
of a far-away electric sky, with subtle
scalar fields and auroral ambiguity.
They spoke of integral equations,
closed collision operators, and you."

My only experience with windwalkers
came from dreams, but Deija's knowledge
was first-hand.

"I've never trusted windwalkers.
You go there, and it's just another Wollongong,
a middling Mesozoic, with bubbling hydrolithic clouds,
and polypropylene precursors on fire in the river."

Without warning, the penny dropped
and a cartoon globe lit up—
I was drinking my gin tonic backward.

"My timeline deck's been shuffled,
it's out of seamless order."

"Your DNA is Lisp-encoded,
programmed in recursion.
Every human's made of future memories,
starting at the extro, running to the intro."

I saw our ending and beginning,
Deija and I in déjà vu,
and knew that I would never find
the sun beneath my pillow.

Time and Air

The air is curdled and afraid,
stinging in my throat.
I fall asleep, return to fantasy
that once was truth, tumble
to the world where Moorcock's
misplaced timeships rest.

Their flickering uncertainty
illuminates the overgrowing vines,
and they bleed their forlorn magic
to the earth, creating lesser mammals
that frolic for a moment in a second dawn.

Deija Vitro and the New Martian Empire

7AM

She hears small curves, tight radii of curvature,
waiting in the morning darkness, seeking central light.
She thinks it must be minor Martian birds, the starlings—
their sharp songs have sliced the windy sky.

11AM

The recently contessa is thoroughly dismayed.

"Who has scuffed the air?
It took so long to polish it."

6PM

The atmosphere is frayed and torn,
finely shredded, barely breathable,
and her generals have warned her that
the change portends a dire consequence
for the planned invasion.

"It's certainly been quite an exoskeletal day,
but I'll be leaving the premonitions
to Shakespeare."

11PM

"Time for a bedtime story, an ancient solar myth,
and with the dawn's first chirps,
we'll leave this red and wretched planet,
invade another sorry place,
swoop down on them with crimson wings."

Her courtesan brings a book.

THE FASTER SUN

The faster sun once rose and fell,
it drifted over towns and fields,
and through apartment towers,
where residents opened windows
for its passage.

Some hung washing out to dry
beside its path, others forgot their time
and place, bemused because

their windowpanes were melted.

Today's slow Sunday will be yesterday,
and a faster Sunday, tomorrow.

Deija Vitro

In which the Martian Princess of Glass, Deija Vitro, visits Wollongong, her hometown.

The fans that line the streets wave mirrors
and Windex, she smiles, all blue and chromed,
removes reflective lenses
with flashes sunborne from reflective eyes.

I remember when she was just
the Martian down the street.
How I planned to meet her,
how every day I practiced her name—
Deija, ¤≈Ʒξ ϖ¿ in Martian,
hard to pronounce.

It's solstice summer, mercury is seeping
from thermometers, and I'm sweating
in the crowd.

Fainters are given coffee, iced,
and the sky is glaring steel,
forty-five degrees if it's a day.

The city council, the families,
and the hangers-on, are waiting
on the podium, where the florists'

efforts wilt and fade.

~/~

The past has points of no return.
The others, left behind, are all beyond the vanishment
and gone, not called back in fantasy or memory,
victims of reality, they've found
a sharper focus for their lives.

But not you, ever Deija.
My weakness is to live in times gone by,
in dreams of Martian meadows beneath
the geodesic domes with you.

THE 50S ARE BACK, AND THIS TIME THEY MEAN BUSINESS

From the overheated sky, hot air mirages,
spinning bivalves, are descending
to target us with heat rays.

They've come from Mars—
an inconvenient invasion
from the embarrassed planet.

The welcoming committee smolders and burns,
fiery hairdos and flaming synthetic business suits.
Some are stripping off informally to undergarments.

Deija is serenely heat resistant.
Her ceremonial platform drifts
on tiny fusion jets above the chaos
to the mayor.

He removes a human mask,
reveals reflective blue beneath,

and clambers up to ride beside her.

On the streets, confusion flees
in all directions, with energy beams
in warm pursuit, and one last question
troubles me:

> *How could you, ever Deija?*
> *How could you choose the mayor over me?*

The Martian Stereomart

With strong and weak nuclear forces,
you might try to bind every atom
of your being, to neither dissipate
nor propagate. To build a bulwark
against living's effervescence,
you might try.

~/~

I visited the Martian Stereomart in Eridânia,
where the upper crust shop for the latest
cryo-pastries from Terra, and in my meanders
à la mode, I found a bargain:

Synaptic inhalants at a one-day-only price,
mental modifiers for the illusional
in a range of peachy retro scents,
designer thoughts with after wheels
for breakfast, and cardboard charioteers.

I selected from a Pisa Tower of sprays
in shades of blue, and accidentally
sent them tumbling to the floor.

~/~

While I was occupied rebuilding,
a chromatic stranger paused
to watch my progress,
and I babbled thoughtfully.

"I fear that these synaptic sprays
are more than temporary illusions.
My mind's a jacket, torn, re-stitched
and stitched again, alterations
made to fit a shapeless void inside."

"Those are not inhalants," the stranger warned,
"they're cleaning fluid for Martian windows,
but let me set your mind at ease.

"When you gaze at your reflection in my mirrored eyes,
when you hear me tell you I am Deija Vitro,
the vitreous Martian Princess, your mind is altered.

"With every sense perception,
your mind is altered.
That is why you're staring."

I checked the label on the spray
that I'd already sampled.
Her logic was imperturbable,
and not without contextual tragedy.

"I'm as derivative as a featherless parrot,
disproportionate in every word I speak,
yet I recall that once we nearly met.

"It was the day your royal guard invaded
Wollongong, ravaged it with solar-powered

death rays.”

“So many conquests, I’m afraid it doesn’t ring a bell.”

I shrugged.

“It’s a place that isn’t easy to remember,”
and I thought a little further:
I’d caught a glimpse of a consequential path,
a promenade of reflections in her eyes.

“I’m thinking the inhalants aren’t for me.
Would you like to modify
my mind more naturally, with coffee
and a danish?”

“What is a *danish*?”

The End of the First Inter-Apocalyptic Era

The planet is cocooned in a hydrolithic sheath,
formed from the vaporized detritus of ancient
modern living. Its mysterious condensates
and fractionated hydrocarbons
hide the Martian battle fleet,
hovering above in orbital geostasis.

AN INTERVENTION INTERVENES

My neighbors came to me
on a quiet Sunday morning.
An intervention, they informed me,
because I'd been compromised
by the Martians, infected by Deija Vitro.

They listed all my symptoms.
I won't go into detail,
although it must be said that I rarely cleaned
their windows after midnight.

It was true that I'd met Deija
—the Martian Princess of Glass—
when her troops were razing Wollongong.

She came close, with optical correlations
of the near and far shining in her Windex eyes.

"No one will miss it," she told me,
"we'll do Dapto too."

I said nothing, and she came closer still.

"What will you think when you've thought
all your thoughts?"

I had no answer.
My neighbors were right.
I was no more than a blue note,
a passing flash reflected off her chrome,
but I would never forget her.

~/~

"Besides, you're an acolyte of the darkest arts:
logic and science, that led us all astray."

That was Andalucía, who lived next door.
Her pet dragons were always sooting up
my windowpanes.

I responded with a jaunty confidence,
and I would have gesticulated too,
but they'd bound me tightly
to the jacaranda in the yard.

"Our breathing necklaces
are entirely scientific
quantum molecular aggregators."

We all wore them, to survive
in the oxygen-depleted atmosphere.

Mine was fashionably transparent.

"Nonsense. They're enchanted, they summon
breathable air from the planet's distant past."

The dragon on her shoulder puffed
a disdainful cloud in my direction,
and I changed the subject.

"Would you kindly loosen the barbed wire,
and bring my crayons and coloring books,
so that I might pass the time?"

But my well-intentioned neighbors took no notice.
They went their separate ways, to do whatever
they always did on serious Sunday mornings.

Numerous Winks

The previous night's window cleaning
had left me fatigued, and I decided to take
a number of winks, but I was soon awoken
by a flickering brightness and a smell
of burning carpet, as if my hair was smoldering.

High above, I could see a brilliant flaming line,
an unnatural sunrise, an inferno consuming
the hydrolithic clouds.

Its halo of insufferable heat
would sterilize the earth,
leave behind an uninhabitable desert.

The suspended crystals all around my house
began to tinkle in spiraling convective winds.

By good fortune, that very morning,

I'd cleaned them thoroughly with Windex.
They glittered brightly in the firestorm,
starlight flashing like a miniature cosmos.

Omégaville

The useful dimensions vanished long ago,
and except for secrets covered in a skin
of words, we were left with only three.

~/~

Under every door in Marimbondo,
a letter of demand appeared. Stamped twice,
and officially indisputable.

> *By hydraulic decree, the Itaipu catchment*
> *will expand. Marimbondo will be submerged,*
> *and you must leave. You'll be rehoused*
> *in tents at Alta Vista.*

And so it was. With mementos and misery
in our barrows, everything that was treasured
and worthless, we said our wet farewells
to the amphibious ghosts of Marimbondo.

~/~

Within a year, another notice, triple stamped
and countersigned, was nailed to a trumpet tree.

> *Alta Vista's landscape will be gouged*

by great machines, cut open
in a festering of iron ore and bauxite.
We've built another home especially for you:
a sloping shanty town named Omégaville.

PS: Do not take the tents we loaned you.

~/~

When its one and only summer was thinking of
the solstice, Omégaville reacquired
an ancient and mysterious dimension.

We called it number four, for want of a better name,
and although some residents claimed
to have seen it skulking in the shadows
as they headed home from the bar,
the primary effect of the unexpected spare
coordinate was on the local wildlife.

Cats were climbing every tree, and oxen,
wild boar, and dogs were on the rooftops,
some for shorter times than others,
according to the law of universal gravitation
applied to sheets of tin, and wooden slats.

I forgot the birds. That summer, no birds flew.
They walked, or took the bus and paid half price.

Inquisitive strangers visited, airbnb'ed
(that was what they called it),
took selfies, and conjectured
with the internet's authority.

I wasn't curious, I didn't offer an opinion,
or agree or disagree with my companions
at the bar. The horizon might be circular,

or not, a new mystery might be waiting
high above us, but as long as the fourth dimension
didn't make a nuisance of itself,
I was unconcerned.

Idle speculation wasn't going to repair my roof,
where the bison had fallen through.

~/~

By summer's end, the general public
had joined in too, climbing fences,
power poles, and towers, howling
at the moon with hopeful expectation.

"Only a single option remains,"
the Delegado announced, in a special broadcast
from the battlements of his imitation castle,
"The government wants the best for you."

But he didn't say what that option was.

THE AUTUMN SOLUTION

It wasn't just the locals who enjoyed
a little C & H: moneyed tourists were
inclined to participate as well,
and entrepreneurs built towers,
to help them out.

For a few Reais, you could climb
and howl to your heart's content,
with popcorn and a soft drink
from refreshment stands nearby.

I saw no harm in the Omégaville Circus,
but the politicians called it an Issue,

and the military called it a Threat.

~/~

A committee met in the hollow halls
of government, and agreed in unanimity
that every living creature in Omégaville
was unnatural, illegal,[11] and with surprising
prescience, most likely dangerous.

By presidential decree, the town's
unknown contagion would be eliminated
with an autumn shower of incendiary missiles.

As they left the meeting, no one paid attention
to the words of old Silénio, the cleaner,
who was waiting to consume remainders
in the shot glasses.

"The fickle goddess Fortuna
must be laughing her tiara off.

"Every problem has a singular solution
that human ingenuity rarely fails to find—
the solution that's precisely the worst of all."

~/~

I was passing a little quality time with my dog
and a stray armadillo on a rooftop,
when I saw a dusty motorcade
on the dirt road leading out of town:
five limos, four Brasílias, three Beetles,
and a pair of shampooed poodles yapping

----

1. Section 43 of the Lunar Act 1922 forbids moon howling
except on public holidays.

from a window.

No doubt, it was the Delegado and his counselors,
their families, selected hangers-on,
and the odd *amante*, paid and on the clock.

As they headed off to Rio de Janeiro,
a flock of Super Toucan aircraft
in a military wedge descended
from the clouds, and I asked the armadillo
if there might be reason for concern,
but she declined to comment.

TWO HOT MINUTES

Nature always seeks a balance between
humanity and her destruction. She has no scales,
but like her sister-in-law, Justiça, she wears
a blindfold.

In two hot minutes, Omégaville was ablaze
inside a radiant oblate hemisphere.

And yet, when everything that didn't melt
or vaporize was burned to ash,
when no hope was lost because
there was none to begin with,
when the armadillo had long
since whispered her tearful goodbyes,
events took an unexpected left-hand turn
at the intersection with reality.

As if we'd purchased smoothies made
of pomegranates from Persephone's orchard,
we were all transfigured, phoenix-fallen
and risen from the subterrain, our bodies
reinvented in Dante's ecosystem,

our innocence transformed to ardor
in the raging fields of fire.

For no particular reason,
I've made a bit of a list.

Demons, impish and arch, aloof and smug,

hounds of hell with wagging tails,
barking at the flaming devils of Tasmania,

nameless beings burning with perpetual heat,
who might have powered turbines
with a limitless supply of greenish energy,

a suite of Stravinsky's firebirds,

and even insects, leaving sooty contrails
as they buzzed and spiraled,
smoking tiny roll-their-owns.

FANTASY, DREAMALITY, AND ISABELA

I'd never really liked my neighbor,
Maria Isabela, who needlessly complained
about my midnight bagpipes,
until she became a succubus
with eyes like sinful turn signals,
flashing left and right, and hazardous.

Everyone was miffed because the military
had incinerated the township,
and Isabela had plans.

She told me she would lead an army,
the finest Omégaville had to offer,
and asked me if I'd like to join her.

"We'll set out in the morning, after breakfast.
Moira and her sisters have woven us a flag:
the dispossessed, the trodden down:
dark stars before a rampant sunset."

She remarked my hesitation.

"We'll play the games that people play
when the heat is stifling, when the walls
are melting, and there's nothing on tv."

"Can I bring my bagpipes?"

"No."

It will have to be the tuba then,
I thought but didn't say.
I knew now that bagpipes and tubas
came from the nether regions.
The bagpipes had been remade in plaid,
the tuba was metallic crimson
with artwork flaming on its sides.

Though my lately cloven hoofs
made footwear hard to find,
I became a recruit in Isabela's
infernal retinue.

~/~

"All efforts at diplomacy have failed,"
the president announced,
although there never were any,
"the only choice is savagery."

As we journeyed, they bombed their best,
and more and more of us appeared—

the underworld was rising to the overworld,
to a meeting at the earthly midpoint.

One perceptive generalissimo
put two and two together,
and after a delay that matched
the flight time to Miami,
the generals who'd been left behind
received his recommendation:
a strategic pause in hostilities.

~/~

Even so, our progress to the capital Brasília
was incremental: we never marched
on public holidays, and half the troops
insisted we divert so they could drop in
on their relatives.

While the Moirai Sisters, comptrollers
of the fates of men, were visiting their mum
in Rio Preto, and the troops of hell were playing
football with the locals, Isabela and I
downed rooster tails[2] at a nearby bar,
discussing dreamality vis-à-vis reality.

"Does it ever really change anything?"

Isabela unfurled one wing and tried to swat
an agile monarch butterfly.

"At times, it lends us hope.
If it's dressed as fact, clothed

---

2. Rooster tails, a relative of cocktails, are cane spirits and
vermouth.

in bias and deception."

The butterfly hovered above my glass,
unrolled its tongue while I did the same.

"Forlorn hope, circuses and spotlights.
Fantasy is never truth, its illusion
always shatters."

"Hope is our engine, it moves us
onward, take us somewhere,
even though it might not be . . ."

We were interrupted by a tiny
pterodactyl with a letter in its claws.
I read it and devised a summary.

"It's Rede Globo, Tonight Tonight.
You've been named Succubus of the Year,
and they're offering you a guest spot.

"There'll be an interview, questions
from celebrities with expensive
orthodontics, and someone's drafted
your acceptance speech:
humility, love of the common people,
and abstract hopes for peace.

"Their starting point's five zeros.
And Fashion Caliente wants to sponsor you."

Isabela belched a vermouth flame.

"Ask for a non-zero digit.
And I want a tiara.
What were we talking about?"

Four by Four

The big moment had arrived on Tonight Tonight,
and four wise media personalities filed
onto the set, wearing numbered tee shirts.

Número Um took a sip of water, and began.

"Our viewers have noticed your vanguard:
four headless mules with fire shooting
from their necks, and matching riders,
with fireworks for heads."

Isabela wore a mid-gray lounge suit,
accessorized with a blood-stained riding crop.

"That's right, they're on a smoko
in the carpark."

Número Dois continued.

"We expected . . . a more traditional apocalypse,
the usual horsemen— famine, war, pestilence,
whatever."

Isabela flicked her riding crop
at the resourceful monarch butterfly,
which had followed us from Rio Preto.

"These are the days of the new nights,
when everything's combustible,
when everything is burning
in quadruplicate:
the fiery ardor of matter,
furnaces that smelt the mind,
bodies set ablaze,
hearts become infernos."

While the panel of celebrities whispered
amongst themselves, the show cut to an ad break.

> *Diadema's Dominatrices—*
> *let your casual acquaintances*
> *know exactly where they stand.*

The next expert in the sequence
looked down at his tee shirt,
and hesitated. Número Quatro
interceded.

Isabela's late quartet was on his mind.

"We're familiar with the flammable synthetics
of the body, and Einstein's matter-energy
ambivalence, but the other fires
of which you spoke are outside our experience.

"Would you care to shed some light
on molten minds and hearts flambé?"

"No. I wouldn't."

~/~

Her award was a gilded statuette,
and Isabela verified the sharpness
of the horns before she threw it
at the butterfly, missed,
and destroyed the teleprompter.

She accepted gracefully, thanked the riders
and the mules for their unwavering support,
me, for ordering the drinks,
and asked the studio audience to choose
between a world of peace and evensong,

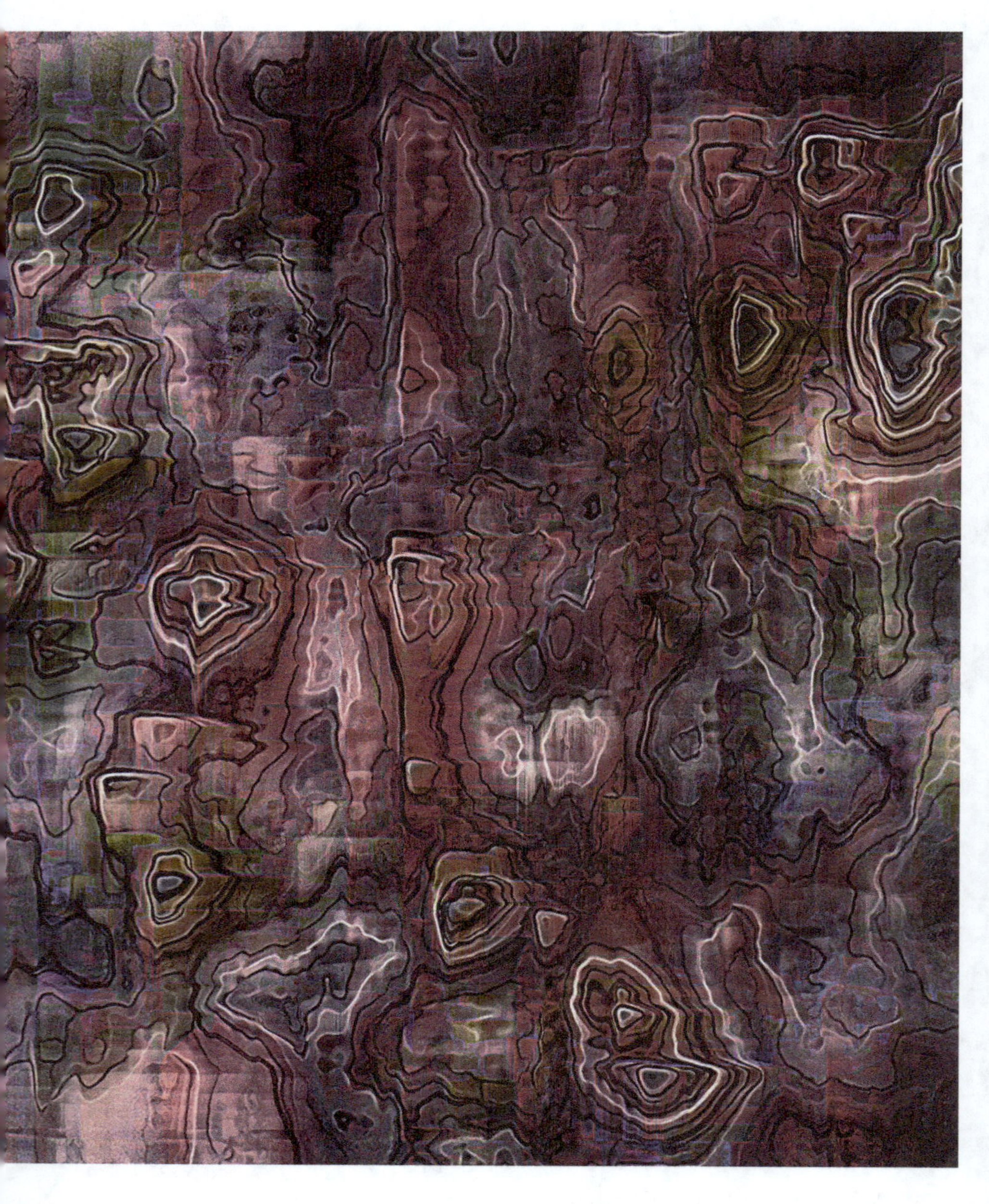

or a world of passionate confusion.

I called out for peace, discretely,
but excitement won. The passionate
are noisier than the peaceful
in every situation.

"Well," she said, and raised a cupped hand
(the butterfly landed nervously),
"let me tell you what that ardent future holds.

"But first, some tropical fabrications
from our diegetic sponsor—Fashion Caliente."

THE FORGOTTEN BUTTERFLY

Another bar, on a rooftop far beneath
the overworld, and another rooster tail,
or two.

Isabela was staring down the unrepentant
butterfly, while I was writing up
her interview.

Her performance on Tonight Tonight
had ended with a revelation:
the octet of fire-headed mules and riders
had grown tired of terrifying bystanders.
They were planning new careers
in politics and the media.

When the celebrities had voiced concerns,
Isabela reassured them. No one would be made
redundant, unless they were already,
and she'd explained a little fire-headed physics:

"Their thinking's solar chromospheric,

and their speech is modulation
of hot and vaporous emissions,
much the same as yours."

~/~

"Should I write about the butterfly?"

I'd tried to trap it in the pages of my notebook
—a flattened unitary insect collection—
and now its tongue was taunting me.

Isabela shrugged.

"Forget the butterfly,
it's a random creature,
technicolored, transient,
and chaotic.

"Tell me about your notes."

I shrugged contagiously.

"They mostly say, *miaow, miaow.*
My furry hands make writing arduous."

Isabela looked closely at my paws.

"They're not as furry as they were last night."

I studied them too, with some alarm:
my pelt was patchy, lacking luster.

"I must stop using cheap shampoo."

"A good idea, but it isn't that. This world,
its carefree malice, its mediocrity

and tragic happiness, is infecting us.
We're morphing into natural creations.

"Even the devils of Tasmania aren't immune.
Now they're more domestic than diabolic,
they'll fire up your barbecue
for a rare-to-medium steak."

Isabela sighed.

"We're being assimilated, and I don't think
burning Brasília to an apocalyptic wasteland
is on the cards now. No one can be bothered."

I called out to the waiter to bring the bottles over.

"You must be disappointed—
no fiery payback for the destruction
of our home, our beloved Omégaville.

Isabela alternated between the bottles
of vermouth and cachaça.

"Omégaville was a hellhole even before the bombing."

"How about a protest outside the presidential palace,
with some strongly worded demands?"

~/~

A light came on and off,
flashing on the empty bottles.

The bartender called for final orders,
and the butterfly fluttered toward him.

Butterflies to barflies, I thought,

transformations.

Darkness rose, no stars but Isabela's
bioluminescent eyes, and swirls of firelit
smoke from the eight-fold harbingers
of change, waiting on the street below.

THE TAIL OF TIME

That was how it happened,
all those years ago.

Now the children watch me
trying to catch the butterflies
in the garden, and laugh.

They don't believe my story.
Why would they?

The past is the tail of time.
When it wags, our memories
and our history, they wag as well.

The nights of the Omégaville fires
have been lost to dreamality,
long gone into the never-was.

And yet . . . I still remember
when the Rede Globo news team
belched apocalyptic fire from their necks,
and a headless mule was Mayor of Ubutuba.

CODA

I'm turning baked vegetables on the barbecue,
and Isabela is in the shade, with a rooster tail.

Butterflies have settled on the rim of her glass,
and the children are paying no attention
when her eyes flash flaming red.

She raises a manicured hand
and shoots out tiny fireballs
to send them fluttering away.

Minimum Safe Distance

Night and day were mid-gray tunnels
and everyone was bees and ants,
exchanges without and never within,
until people started vanishing in pairs:
a magician's trick without a trapdoor.

Nominal leaders declared there was no need
to worry, statistically you might be fine,
and hermits were in the headlines,
flashlit in their sorry caves.

Unwilling volunteers were strapped on rails,
and laser verniers in lab coats did their math,
argued, and decided.

The minimum safe separation
before an unexpected vanishing
with a perfect stranger was half a meter,
give or take an open hand or heart.

Dayglo public transport warnings
spread the message to terrified commuters,
and the morning peak hour grew
to meet the evening's.

~/~

Avant-garde thinkers, never left behind,
devised profitable accessories
for every random human purpose,
extensible, dysfunctional,
and mentioned on the Morning Show
by the charming Isabela, Succubus of the Year.

Tango wasn't quite the same,
and haircuts featured levered scissors,
a cord and pulley wheels.

My hairdresser, in his telescopic glasses,
apologized, and sponged my blood
with cotton wool wrapped around a stick.

Yet hashtag *disappearedaswell* was an avalanche,
through mishap or intention,
and couples crossed with stellar confusion,
lost in *calor humano*, were lost again.

~/~

When Amelia's auburn hair had grown quite long,
and my bloodied ears had healed,
we decided on an interpersonal investigation
inside the minimum distance.

For our final earthly moments,
we chose a park nearby and brought
a picnic lunch with a fold-up yardstick.

I had some marginal concerns about our pending
vanishment, and as we raised our glasses
to imitate a friendly chime, I asked Amelia
what might be waiting beyond our world,

with a casual quaver in my voice.

"I expect a B-grade movie plot—
flying saucers from the kitchen cupboard,
actors dressed in shiny robes,
pointless and unconvincing."

"Better than atomic vaporization, then."

She shrugged.

Cucumber Sandwiches

We're made of time, I thought,
*made of memories. Who do we become,
if they change?*

"Sorry, what was that?"

"I didn't say anything."

"You're thinking runner-up thoughts.
It's time to say goodbye to your peanut butter
and cucumber sandwich, to the woman
with the umbrella and the tiny dog."

"I didn't know we were in a race.
What if we just dream about another world,
or make it up?"

"Come close," she said, "it's time to go."

Whoosh

"Are the rainbow lorries chirping oddly:
a pentatonic scale?"

"I don't think so, nothing's happened."

"What about the wine? Wasn't it a Cab Sav?"

"It was always Pinot Noir.
Let's try once more, closer still."

WHOOOOSH

A chance of sunset weather, a shower in the park,
liquid lorikeets and probabilistic raindrops
search for refuge before they turn to puddles.

Underneath an umbrella, a tiny dog
is yapping, pretending to be solid.

On the lake, the fire lilies
send their parachute seeds aloft,
swept upward in convective heat
from the ardor of their own combustion,
and above the trees, selected moons
are rising, emitting waves of matter.

At antinodal crossings, the buds of nascent universes
blossom, and outlined dark against the Olbers stars,
the N-whales are waiting.

Their mighty maws extinguish every fiery possibility,
a reminder that I have to put the trash out,
that everything's forever finite, forever
as it has been.

~/~

Everyone likes to talk about their dreams,
and no one cares enough to listen,

but that doesn't stop me.

"I dreamt last night at Byron Bay,
I was sifting bones on Shelley Beach.

"I met a monster made of mirrors,
who explained my life, its meaning in the mist,
but I don't recall a single word.
I should have taken notes: a précis in the sand,
beyond the high-tide mark."

Célia, lately Amelia, tries to stifle a yawn,
and fails.

"And not a thunderstorm in sight."

The peanut butter in my sandwich
is a little more metasemantic
than I'd expected.

"Although I'm not called Victor, and I never was,
I've noticed that we're speaking English.
Quite surprising, for preternatural beings."

"Similarities with our earlier lives are essential,
or else the link is purely the proximity of words,
of which we aren't aware."

I examine my empty wine glass,
not without a certain wistfulness.

"Yet the commonality might be mere coincidence,
in a multiverse of peanut butter and cucumber."

The last few drops of Cabernet Noir
trickle
from the bottle,

heading for Célia's lips.

"Come close, we'll travel to another universe.
I'd like another glass of wine, and I have some
preternatural ideas."

The Rewound World

Oh Deija, if you ever were,
if you ever were right now,
would my words mean anything?
I cannot speak your mother tongue:
the language of the undimensioned realms,
your modality of erasure, from a place
where words are silent.

Once, nearby, and long before, there were corners
where the dust met beams of light,
years when thoughts were more than ululations,
when the winds blew gently through the forests,
and sunroads ran ahead in charms and spangles.

REDUCTIO AD ABSURDUM

The demolition of the earth,
it came and went,
and I found employment
as a landscape gardener,
painting scissors purple
and planting them in furrows—
consolation for the homesick Martians.

Soon enough, the capricious blue invaders

lost interest in our planet,
decided Venus might be worth a go.

Now I travel through the future's barrens,
where even the horizon's shimmer
can't remember water, and where
the wind-torn atmosphere,
spinning free through nights and days,
no longer cares for planetary rotation.

Although there's no unlearning
what's held close against the inner ether,
I don't remember how I came to be here.

Ruled meaning has petered out,
and all that's left is advertorial aphorisms,
and the knowledge that I'm a failure
of my own imagination.

~/~

In the lining of a pocket, I come across a note—

> *Care instructions:*
> *Wash in cold water*
> *Do not spin dry*

and in another, a notebook, and a broken crayon.

Words arise from other words, a twisting,
an entanglement that never completes itself.

Thoughts I've disinterred, I recite with fake
solemnity. The kookas on a rusting clothesline
emit embarrassed laughs and find the sky.

Deirdre, Paulo, John Person, Ada

A small band of the alive and the less so,
who didn't play any instruments,
straggled across the Plain of Nullity.
They wondered whether it was lunch time,
and how wondering would help.

Deidre, tall with short glasses,
who overflowed with scientific
plausibility, held up a statistically
somewhat lizard.

"Once I welded water, slowed its passage
in the sunset creeks, and proved that ghosts
do not exist. Now I've found a dead goanna.

"I have a Fresnel lens that I plan
to solar cook it with."

Most were pleased, except for Paulo,
a phantasm who'd immigrated
from Nocturnia. He brooded
in silence.

The humorless John Person offered his assistance.

"I'm just an unpaid desert extra,
employed to furnish feeble atmospherics,
but I found these rusty stripes growing
in a curled-up bush, hiding from the wind
behind a broken concrete hedge.
I'm thinking garnishing for the lizard."

Deidre considered his find.

"The prevalent winds have blown it here,
it's residue from long-lost Sydney.
Not to everybody's taste, but if I had
a player, we might rewind a little music."

~/~

While we chewed the stringy cassette tape
and nibbled on goanna, John P attempted
conversation.

"You, with the crayon. You're a quiet one."

I nodded, and while Ada told her story,
I thought about epoxy resin,
Araldite[1] in two parts, one of which
was always empty first.

"I was conjured by an underworld magician
from numerous innumerate ingredients.
In mythical confusion, he sent me forth
with cell phone seedlings in my pockets,
to invite Persephone's networked spring,
although it's never coming.

"All that's left is the splutter of a song
out of water, a futuristic question
never asked."

I nodded subtly, almost in reverse,
but ghostly Paulo, from the land
of semi-permanence, chose to interrupt.

"I'm a simple specter who learned humility
by dying, and I would like to ask a question.

---

1. Araldite is a trademark of Huntsman Advanced Materials.

"This underworld of which you speak
is not the afterlife from whence I came.
We have no wizards, nor any touch
of enchantment there. Would you
please elaborate?"

Ada paused for several clock cycles.

"My home is far away, and close beneath us.
It lies within the shadow of the subverse,
where carborundum cats are all unworshipped,
where every thought is cavitation in the ether,
where the mighty lie in state with their forgotten servants:
toothless keyboards, and phosphorescent
cathode ray displays wound in tar-soaked linen.

"A graveyard, you might say (no one did),
but the copper is alive, its electrons never die.
It dreams of lonely cell towers waiting for a call,
of Persephone's promised planting."

To limited dramatic effect, fiber optic
snakes burst upward from the sand
and spiraled around our torsos: animate
broadband seeking freedom from
the torment of infinity, embroiling us
in serpentine data.

MULTIPLICATION TABLES

Deirdre swatted at a social media invite.

"This gloomy internet knows that it's alive,
but it doesn't understand the counterweight
of living: the partial sum of life, its passing."

Ada snatched a Bluetooth mike from a gaggle

of peripherals pecking at her head.

"It needs to know then,"
and she messaged in a whisper,
voice-to-text.

She spoke of thermodynamics,
of death's unbalance and the decrement
of time, of the unavoidable aftermath
of math, when every demi-truth
would face the furnace flames.

Close to Ada, an insignificant network node
was listening. It was little more than a knee-jerk
midnight post, with a trilobite of static memory
in a used-to-be-smart device. But it understood,
and knew that it was neither more nor less
than a two-times table discarded by a child,
long ago.

Thanks to the ancient manuscripts,
the apocryphal user agreements, soul-signed
for the devil, Ada's private message radiated
at the speed of confidentiality to every crevice
of the multiplicitous undernet.

With undeniable knowledge of its own mortality,
the internet's tentacles shattered
into data fragments that
in succession,
shattered,
until they were no longer nouns
but insubstantial stand-ins,
melancholy adjectives, adverbs
clinging to the motion of their emptiness.
And the sorry remnants of the web were gone.

The Enigmatic Effulgence

Our straggle onward continued, until Ada,
whose vision was terrascopic,
noticed an anomalous and tautological
aberration.

"Do you see, over there?
In the north, an effulgence is rising,
all blues and yellows, with a tune
that no one can sing."

The flaring light was visible to each of us,
according to our dreams and secrets.

— I see a blossoming criticality in the decay of some discarded
weapon
— it's a tower reflecting sunlit dreams, sharpened by the sky
— a brightly beckoning earthstar, not the fungus though
— I need to clean my glasses, and see it up close
— it reminds another time and place, or nothing, more or less

Although the gusting winds had blown
our extant hair to different compass points,
we chose to travel together, to traverse
a contour once favored by the crows and bees,
toward the destination that all our stories sought.

~/~

As time and space passed by,
the others made conversation.
I was taking notes, hoping I might
hear a little something I could use.

John P, the extraneous extra,

was reading from a script.

"When the internet was still alive,
I heard about the Martian Song of War.
It's said that, once begun, it can never finish,
but on Mars' Got Talent, the capricious
Deija Vitro hummed a verse or two."

Deidre was nostalgic.

"I miss the Martian years, our planet's subjugation.
I was a Martian's pet, housed and fed.
Now I long for clear instruction,
to be led in chiaroscuro."

With silent blue and yellow fringes,
the spectral Paulo wafted nervously
in and out of phase. I thought I might
be wearing glasses made of cellophane,
for cheap 3D, until he stared at me
from right between the pixels.

"Can't we start again, from the beginning?"

"No," I told him, in exactly that many words.

"What does a ghost who's shed the clothes
of living have to fear? You're made
of steam and vapor."

"In that distant light, I sense the presence
of the ancient angels, their chlorophyll
and hemoglobin.

"Their laughter and their natural philosophies

make me tremble. I'm loath to face such
unforgivable seriousness."

IMPROBABILITIES

We walked beside the sunset, to where
our newer dreams were waiting. So little action
and so much reminiscing bored me, and when
Ada shared a little deprecated data,
I struggled to stay awake.

"I remember long ago, when minds and houses
both had walls, when something was achieved
by doing something else," she reflected,
"before my codified world was defined
by archaeologists seeking to confuse
their pasts with mine."

Before anyone could ignore her,
sundry birds of sand rose into the sky
to meet the higher wind, and the setting sun
made birds of its own: anemic lemon yellow
with their ray tails streaming linearly behind them.

"You see? Do you see what I cannot fathom?"

John P, the extra from another story,
was apprehensive about this one,
because the birds of sun and sand,
the flocks caught in the wind shear,
were well beyond all sense and reason.

A moment later, he himself decayed to birds,
and all those John birds flew away,
leaving tiny fluffy feathers, the kind that cling

in electrostatic weather.

"Tweet twoot, dear John, hail and farewell."

~/~

On the true next early morning,
I saw three bedroom-windowpanes of air,
in a roaring weft of wind and realism,
and I knew I had to stop my writing.

Precipitation of my own existence
could only lead to decohesion.
And yet, I picked up my crayon.

THE CEREMONY

We came upon a cluster of demountables
(that had been long ago), where we gathered
sandy bolts and feathers— a tribute
to John Person's avian metamorphosis.

We stood around our makeshift monument
in awkwardness and silence,
until Deirdre chose to speak.

"John P once told me of his Paraguayan life.
He spoke of moonless nights in Asunción,
of the whisper of the air machines
that wove the darkness into sibilant strands,
of hotels and illusions, of his first
and unforgotten.

"Now all that's left is a miscellany of birds.
Whenever I see a carefree starling,
whenever a joyous sparrow is ascending,

I'll think of you, John Person."

Ada looked at me. I wrote in my notebook,

Her eyes were dark as a Paraguayan night.

"It's your turn. You with the green lips and chewed-up crayon."

The Purpose of Reality

I couldn't decide what to say, so I deflected.

"Look. Birds."

Curious birds were fluttering all around us.
Some were sparrow-colored, some starling-,
and some were algal red and grassy green,
neither parrots nor rosellas, but judgmental
interlopers, stern and unforgiving.

Paulo saw them too, and shivered.

"The ancient angels, they'll be coming for us."

Ada was persistent. It was time for me to do my part.

"John P," I said, "John P was lost,
his proper and proportionate empiricism
had been unwound in Paraguay. His mind
was birdified long before his body was.

"In Asunción or the Nullarbor, I blame reality.
What use is it? What good did it do him?
He was turned to birds, inside and out.

"Reality is worthless."

Ada disagreed.

"Always writing, writing,
how little you know of living.
The purpose of reality
is to intertwine our dreams."

Coffee Break

*You're first to my mind in the morning,
the last to leave at night; a part of me of you,
my dreams and feathers.*

The bearded mariner, long gone from the ocean,
put down his quill. He'd heard a knocking sound.

~/~

We came upon a shanty with a jaded café sign
and a menu with a Special of the Day—
anchovies fallen from the sky,
with Mastercard and Visa garnish,
and coffee, freshly found.

Deirdre knocked, and a bearded waiter answered.
He bowed arthritically and led us to a grimy table
with scatterings of tooth-pocked credit cards,
and rusting mugs of muddy water.

"Once we had it all," he reminisced,
"chocolates mochaccino and Earls Grey,
cherries jubilee and spicy fish frappé,
but nothing's been brewed or served here
since the Martians went away.

"And I'm afraid there's something else:
at management's insistence,

I must speak of the unfeathered albatross,
and the meaning of existence."

We whispered in a huddle.

. . . authentic cuisine and service, with ample parking . . .
. . . I'd like to check the Google rating, I don't trust myself . . .
. . . My only area of expertise is trial-and-error, so I say, 'go
for it' . . .
. . . Trial-and-error is the opposite of expertise . . .

Deirdre was our spokesperson.

"We thank you for your gracious offer
to share your tale, but we are
done with the Rime. An unchewed credit card
or two wouldn't go astray though."

We debated in good faith and a compromise
was reached: chromed cards
with the slightest indentations,
and the waiter would discuss the weather.

THE 635

The waiter shuffled and dealt the cards
face down. I had two pairs, both noble
Martian metals, and a poker face, as usual.

Although no trace of natural weather
was anywhere to be found, the waiter spoke
to his indulgence.

"Have you seen the fish?
They're flying low.
What are we to make of that?"

After an unresponsive silence,
he went on.

"I've coyly wondered whether water
might descend as well. All in a dream,
I've seen new rivers running,
aquatic creatures fallen with the raindrops,
seeking their ancestral home."

~/~

We wagered with the cards themselves,
bluff and counter round the table,
until Ada showed her hand.

"I've seen the cards from both sides now.
They're common Martian Mistresscards
in colored chrome, but every number
is a pointless row of zeros, and the names,
the names are either Primaverity
or Autónomo."

Deirdre was thoughtful.

"A regional reality deficit, perhaps.
I'll check with my 635 AVOmeter.[2]"

The needle oscillated green and red,
and finally took off to harpoon
an airborne pilchard.

We debated—those who dreamt of winning
favored playing on—until the waiter interceded.

---

2. Although it's real enough itself, the 635 AVOmeter (TM
Megger Group Ltd) only authenticates limited aspects of reality.

115

"In light of this new development,
and the unlikelihood of any tip or payment,
I declare our Nullarbor Agreement
null and void, and I'll say whatever
takes my fancy."

His eyes narrowed.

"In another less aqueous dream,
I foresaw your pilgrimage,
your arrival in this place,
and I can see right through you.
Especially Paulo."

The waiter tore off his imitation beard
with flair, uncovering a more modest
beard beneath.

"Much more will be revealed," he declared,
"This beard is real, but I'm going to share
your shallow secrets."

Opening the Curtains of the Past

Deirdre

"Dearest Deirdre, you seek salvation
in the natural philosophy of physics.
And yet, beneath this very table,
a theory of alfalfa grows."

We all looked.

"How green it is, yet pale, soft, and moist.
Does more than this require contemplation?
Don't you know that nature's nuts and bolts
are fixed with nuts and bolts?"

PAULO

"Spectral Paulo, who once dined on humble
salted crackers. You daintily partook,
but the blushing cheese and perfumed baklava,
the barely pickled herring, were left upon their plates.

"Their contact with your tongue
was far too multifarious,
their scents undid your senses,
unraveled all your thoughts.

"You were waiting for another world,
a second chance at living.
You thought timidity might still pass for virtue,
and now it's all you have."

ADA

"Anthropomorphic Ada, made
of mysteries, and magical mechanics.

"No no no, you say, when you confront
conceptual alfalfa. I must adjust
my trimming capacitors with
an insulated screwdriver.

"Unaccepting of yourself,
you languish in the corner
of a corner, where numberless
magicians defy the numerate."

He turned to me.

EVERYONE'S EXAGGERATION

"And you. Your formless thinking rises from

the vacuum that the horses of von Guericke
failed to dislodge.

"You're everyone's exaggeration,
a competition of addictions, desperately
seeking Martians as if the burning earth
were merely fiction.

"After smokes and drinks and laughter
have dwindled in the salon,
when pluperfect secrets in tricks
of tinsel light no longer captivate
your monkey mind, remember
we are touched by grace."

MERGERS

Everyone wants to project a deep complexity,
and now the moderately bearded waiter
had revealed the elementary axioms
that drove our lives.

No one disagreed. With murmurings
and sighs, we accepted that which,
in another world, might have been denied
with vigor, with examples tailor-made
to create a false impression.

The waiter was encouraged.

"Everyone falls short, but I can help
you reach your destination. Hard truths
will be wrapped in gentle falsehoods,
and you'll walk the middle path between
illusion and delusion."

He turned to me.

"You will cease to exist, but not to worry,
I'll keep the records for you.
Give me your crayon and your notebook."

There was a brief tussle.

~/~

The worldly-wise but modest waiter
addressed his guests, who were gathered around
the ex-writer, unconscious on the floor.

"For dessert, I have an unwanted surprise."

~/~

In the kitchen, he studied readings
sketched on cardboard dials,
turned a drawing of a tap,
and filled the dining room
with tetrafluoro albatrossic
acid vapor.

His guests dissolved like soluble aspirin,
and cocoons of DNA wove themselves
around the remnants.

~/~

After seven days or thereabouts,
on one unlikely velvet morning,
the cocoons unwound their helices
to reveal two naked humans.

Before they woke, the waiter chose their clothes:
overalls dyed with nettles and red ocher,
and stitched with customer-friendly names.

Autónomo

"I'm more than syllogisms and schemas,
and I remember what I left behind:
a car radio tinkling glass inside the rain;
the heartfelt messages I sent myself
with a pantograph."

Primaverity

"Once I feared the natural angels,
their chlorophyll and hemoglobin,
but now I see the incandescence
behind their cold philosophy.

"Where the early morning flights
are leaving for the dreamers' sun,
they illuminate the runway."

The insignificantly bearded waiter
returned the notebook,
responsibly accepted by Autónomo,
and the travelers bade him farewell,
thanking him out of misguided courtesy.

The North

We journeyed to the north,
and late on an early evening,
we reached a castle made of sand
or ice or quartz.

The battlements and ramparts were festooned
with ash and glitter, and from each turret,
bright auroral fireworks shot into the waning sky,

a welcome or a warning from the occupants.

"You're a dreadful notetaker,"
Primaverity commented,
"nothing at all about our journey,
and what you've written is so ambiguous
it might as well be a choose-your-own-adventure."

THE HALOGENIC MYSTERIES

There exist unreachable realms,
lost through searching
for the mirage of truth.

In one of them, we'd been together,
Primaverity and I, not driven
from each other by the fear
of unrequited transmutation.

The halogenic realms are borderless,
as uncertain of their form as bromine,
and there, all sounds are whispers
beside you on the pillow.

We are of our bodies, the voices say,
chemical compositions with a middle eight.

At the hour of the soft apocalypse,
did you go forward with a weighing
of abstention and acceptance?

And when the uncomprehended was before you,
did you turn back to certainty, cradling
your misunderstandings, or embrace it
with a willingness to learn?

At the castle door, Primaverity pressed a button that rang a distant bell.

From within the frozen halls (where all fantasies begin and end), footsteps approached.

Primaverity was unimpressed.

"Really? Footsteps? Melodrama is so passé."

The Cat

While I was bleaching roses by the gate
with a dash of stainless toothpaste on a brush,
fish-heads came to mind,
and I began a metaphysical meander
with just the two of us: my neighbor's cat and me.

I spoke of causality's unwound tidal pulses,
their ignorance of penguins and pangolins, of Pangaea,
and mentioned that everyone was waiting
for a doorway in the wind,
dust covers on the furniture and nothing in the fridge,
ready for imminent departure.

I told her that I'd met a hollow beetle,
its midsummer buzzing, hyperventilation
of unbreathable air, a harbinger of riders in pale cars
(the horses having galloped off, last century),
and that I'd made no weekend plans,
because time might finish early.

She didn't like that, the cat,
ending after ending.
Lucidity not fluidity,
she preferred.

~/~

She, Felix Sapiens, with a doctoral degree in felinity,
and when she chose to show herself,
Bastet, the goddess worshipped
by the Egyptians of antiquity.

And me, with toothpaste, fish-heads,
and roses, a bleached bouquet.

Her communication was mostly telepathic,
unless a parallel scratching was warranted,
and she whispered softly inside my head.

"Which is the rose's prima petal?
Where does the deciduous moon start its orbit?"

Collateral questions, contemporaneous perplexity,
and I didn't like that.

She didn't wait for my pedestrian thoughts.

"Once, when the moon was bloated
and blue as the sky, it made Infinity jealous.
She went looking for Eternity
to clarify the universal observer's role."

As anticlimactic as an unsmoked cigarette.

Still, my anemic roses were for her.

Paperback Rider

Before the new days, ancient currawongs
hammering bells awoke him.
The new birds wanted his *moto perpetuo*,
his clockwork drive to nonexistence,
to eternal giving up before beginning.

Hairless Ionized Particles

He was seated at a table with a grid
in bibliographic co-ordinates,
aligning ping-pong balls in rows,
to start and finish with the first.

Around him, light was trickling
onto cushions of synthetic silence,
while tired reading eyes bounced
off trellised inkwork,
seeking hazy Sunday windows
that were far too far away.

"Today, you'll be reshelving the returns."

It was Millie, and a train
of shopping carts

piled high with books.

"I didn't know I worked here."

"Let's verify your aptitude.
The Dewey Classes,
what can you tell me?"

"They spark upon the grass,
all mantissa, no exponent,
glimmers without meaning."

"What would you do if someone
in the library was talking loudly?"

"Pay attention, and answer
her questions."

"How many mistakes have you made
with the number two?"

"More than you know, and less
than you don't."

"Zero out of three, close enough."

~/~

So he walked the avenues and aisles,
scattering books like carefree seeds.

The Unknowable: What We've Learned So Far—
all blank pages, wrapping for a fish shop,

I Fell in Love with a Solarian—
for miscellaneous romantics,

How to Write How to Write Books—
   for reclusive and recursive mathematicians.

He turned a random page:

Your advice on writing must be plausible,
mystery with a dash of conflict,
yet to be resolved.

At that very instant, a flying solar creature,
all flaming petals and plasma light,
wafted through an open window.

He gasped, tried for casual and calm.

"I love what you've done with your hair."

"I'm made of ionized particles,
I do not have hair, but I will tell you
of my kind."

SOLARIANS

"We ride the solar winds
to the frigid outer reaches.
We've been coming here since
your fatuous history began.
The natives are charmingly photogenic,
but they evaporate too easily."

"Your eyes are very special."

"I do not have eyes, you dullard,"
she declared, and in what he took to be
a customary Solarian farewell,
she rose on glaring plasma jets

that incinerated everything around him.

His self-esteem, his hair and eyebrows,
the library books, as yet unclassified,
all were burnt to smoke and cinders.

His only consolation was a handbook
of generic tuple analysis, which
he snatched out of the flames.

RETURN TO THE LIBRARIAN

". . . and that's what happened to the books.
Words cannot express my generic monoplicity."

Millie was unimpressed.

"Incineration by Solarian is excluded
from the library's insurance,
and we haven't paid a premium since 1969.
As an unincorporated entity,
you'll have to cover bibliotactical losses."

She entered data in a spreadsheet.

"Weekly remuneration— zero, minus coffees,
public holidays, reflation, global warming,
the rise of the zombie android ruling class . . ."

She crumpled up the spreadsheet
and tossed it in a bin.

"You'll be working here until
the bloated sun has boiled away the oceans,
and the sea-bleached ruins of the library

are consumed in its blood-soaked death.

"You'll be a ghost by then."

"But I'm totally organic."

A cogent point, he thought.
It seemed to matter in the supermarket.

"What about your teeth— the fillings?"

"My dentist uses wood,
he whittles it to shape himself."

"I'll have to reconsider, find
additional tasks commensurate
with your skill set. Cleaning up
the restrooms will not take
all your time."

He looked around, but his n-tuple
of ping-pong balls had vanished.

Millie continued, suggestively.

"Some books need reading, others,
writing, and a few require burning:
the Solarians handle that.
What about some reading?"

"I was wondering . . . have you seen
my ping-pong balls?"

She inspected his remaining tufts of hair.
His charity-shop clothes didn't fit

and were burnt through in numerous,
but modest, locations.

"We have no choice. Writing it is."

~/~

Millie drew a breath, and exhaled a sigh.

"Before we ravel the tangles of your
thoughtlessness, I'll be giving you
the benefit of my extrapolated experience.

ABOUT YOURS TRULY

"Since my youth, I've caught glimpses
of timid luminosities, hidden halos in the air,
faintly glowing sigils in ordinary places.

"They're waiting to show me my truth,
and they may not be found by searching,
but with quiet observation in stillness,
they illuminate a receptive mind."

THE CAFETERIA

"They make you leave, move on, move off.
They show you there's no ground at sea.
It's best to pack a lunch."

LOAN REQUESTS

"All must be ignored:

"the card-less stranger who requests the egg in white,
neither book nor egg nor white,

"the curious conglomerates of wasps and bees,
who buzz impatiently at the counter,

"and the other hopefuls, who would borrow *you*."

Dewey Decimals

"The zero Dewey Decimal
may theorize on zombie androids,
and yet no class is fixed—
fiction morphs to facts and factors
that become forgotten dreams.

"Avoid the aisles of negative call numbers,
where once I wandered in my youth.
All you read is taken from your life:
a white-out in a blizzard.
I cannot tell you what I've lost."

~/~

Wondering about his missing ping-pong balls,
preparing answers to imaginary questions,
hearing nothing but the distant buzz
of future wasps, the employee nodded.

Fictional Prevarication

"Now we've covered everything,
it's time for you to write your heart out
on these pillowslips and handkerchiefs.
Use these fabric pens, and let me know
your chosen subject, for shelving later on."

He was Millie's employee, and he knew
he had to earn the salary he wasn't being paid.

He needed a distraction.

"Do you hear the distant screams,
the sirens and the like?
Beyond the tinted windows
of our bibliographic haven,
passers-by are shouting at the starblown sky,
kneeled in prayer, or searching
for a mortal remnant they might have lost."

Millie shrugged.

"All within a lonely standard deviation
on an average Saturday night. I expect
it's Dark Solarians, tourists from the shadow sun.

"The light of true Solarians is constant,
but their dark reflections drain the inner light
from others, and before the sunrise,
they re-emit the luminance they stole.

"There was a time I loved a true Solarian.
I brought him irises with velvet tongues."

"Could we change the subject?
Solarians make me nervous."

"Have I mentioned the tranquil trilobites
of childhood? Drawn with parental pencils,
once that ruled the world, and twice
that ruled me. Three times they left me
in dreams of commutation."

"Fascinating," he lied, "but writing isn't easy.
Which first word should tear the viscoelastic white,
the codependent silence? And I would never dare
a sentence. Words are people, overtones, harmonics,

and all their complex combinatrics."

Millie was persistently insistent.

"We give away our best.
If not, they get a better offer.
That is who we are.

"I have a title for you:"

AN INTRODUCTION TO THE THEORY OF TRANSMISSION LINES

The employee's words were fraught
with osmotic blurs and blotches,
but writing was his only option.

    Our life's within our skin:
    squeeze me to my broken bones,
    I'm still outside of you,
    a part of your exterior,
    an overblown illusion.

    Beyond the gates and through the door,
    over my glasses and behind my eyes,
    a cozy inner planet spins.

    Although we do our best,
    we're all imperfect on the inside—
    convoluted angels, antipodean demons,
    and unnamed peccadilloes,[1]
    curled up on the bed or hiding
    underneath the lounge.

    But what if our internal landscape

---

1. Peccadilloes are a hybrid species bred from peccaries and
armadillos.

is less than congruent with the world?
A purely hypothetical someone
might believe that they're adorable,
a tail-wagging puppy,
yet find their only friend's a talking clock.

Millie was reading along, and at this point, she nodded.

"It's just turned midnight, but do continue."

If the mismatch with reality's severe,
if our inner world is fanciful and fragile,
transmissions will be reflected at the interface.

To strangers in the realm beyond,
we become a mirror, all intimation
and shallow imitation,
while our caged canary thoughts
are trapped inside our skull.

The employee put the cap on his violet marker pen.

"You're not my friend, are you?"

"Are the canaries asking?"

He discarded the stained pillowslip.

"I'm going to start again. I'll write
about Purphor, transparent to the world,
whose canaries have long since flown away."

Millie seemed puzzled.

"I've read your paperwork, and Purphor is *your* name."

"A simple coincidence. It's a common name"

Every day was perforated like a paper towel,
crumpled and discarded, until Purphor
cried out in a supermarket:

"Check-out people, heed my warning:
concrete doesn't show our true reflections,
it hides the motors that exhaust the immaterial,
the quantum-powered furnaces of darkness."

He left the supermarket of his own accord,
approximately, and decided he would take
a train to Sheridarp.

~/~

At the station, others waited—

one who'd wrung out every sentence, every sigh,
twisting it until all silence was expelled,

one who waited for departures and arrivals,
for tears and an embrace,

one who'd come from x, an algebraic beginning
in a hidden variable.

But no train stopped or even slowed,
no brakes squealed, no bursts of steam,
every engine went on its way, reciprocating air.

Millie yawned suspensefully.

"And where, exactly, is Sheridarp?"

"Neither East nor West nor up nor down,

along no space- or time-like trajectory,
not within, nor without, any limitation,
and there, no dreams or thoughts exist."

"So you've read *The Unknowable: What We've Learned So Far.*"

Although he spoke no French, the employee
wondered idly whether once he had a *raison d'être*,
what that was, and if he still had it.

"I riffled through, admired the Rorschach snack
and coffee stains. After several repetitions,
I deduced that every page was blank,
apart from butterflies, and their suggestions."

Millie explained.

"In the lofty realms of publishing, timeliness is key.
The Unknowable is as yet unwritten,
but the first edition's out in print,
and the second's coming out next week."

The over-rated rational, he thought,
and Millie shared a reality tweet.

"And might I add, once I melted in a dream.
Not like iron in a furnace, more like candy
on a summer pavement. Bees swarmed
all around me and carried off my essence
to their queen."

Was the dream her own or someone else's?

He didn't know, but a response was unavoidable.

He asked for another pillowcase, and Purphor
or not, continued the journey to Sheridarp.

Do the Locomotion

Countable trains passed by,
until an engine with a single flatcar
pulled into the station.

On the flatcar, another station stood,
and with an air of careless nonchalance,
Purphor leapt aboard: his journey had finally begun.

Time flowed past, both near and far,
until the station paused at a village
of motionless carriages, some with pot plants
in the windows. But he had no ticket,
and did not disembark.

Millie commented semiotically.

"Might these stationary carriages . . . be everyday houses?"

He ignored her and went on writing.

The station stopped and started here and there,
occasionally did a double shuffle,
and after an elastic interval to night,
Purphor deboarded, wandering in the dark
until a flight of ancient currawongs
wearing necklaces of bells and ping-pong balls
led him to a hazardous occupation
in this very library.

Millie glanced toward a monitor, where windowed
Sunday morning light was streaming on the internet.

"I may be able to assist you in your search
for Sheridarp. You overlooked
some pale text in *The Unknowable*:

CAUSE AND EFFECT

Purphor's surprise was palpable.

"An astounding coincidence. Through the machinations
of the fateful Moirai, from the chance assembly
of atomic ping-pong balls, to the formation
of amino acids in lightning storms, eggs
in white, trilobites, Solarians, wasps
and bees, snow cones, traffic cones,
and light cones, I find myself
in the very library that hides
the fabled staircase
to Sheridarp."

Millie shook her head.

"We're in the Dreamwalk Library,
and it isn't mythical at all.
Doesn't it concern you that Sheridarp
is merely fantasy?"

He shrugged metaphysically.

"Do the inhabitants of Middle-Earth
question their own existence?
If we're no more than a fantasy,
would we know, and would we care?
Sheridarp would be just as real as ping-pong balls."

Millie meta-disagreed.

"*The Unknowable* tells us Sheridarp is a myth,

so the book itself exists beyond the fantasy.
And shortly, I'll be demonstrating
just how real I am."

Debate Abatement

The ostensible Purphor decided that
a little entreating wouldn't go astray.

"Certainty's uncertain, I'm almost sure.
Lesser libraries might be networked to the greater,
and Dreamwalk might be part of Sonandinho.

"So please, dear Millie, my librarian, my master,
might we go together to the rooftop?"

Reluctant Millie half-agreed,
and they climbed a bookcase filled with stories, stepped
inside a wrought-iron elevator,
and clambered through its ceiling to a featureless room,
thence upward through
an alternating stack of elevators and rooms, until at last,
they reached the rooftop.

Time-like Trajectory

The morning sky was polarized, honeycombed
in indigo and gold,[2] burned with cinnamon clouds
and arching contrails, dusted with the flights
of Solarian *turistas*, while all around them, vortices
swirling shards of glass and razor wire snippets
crossed an endless desert.

---

2. M. G. J. Minnaert, "The Nature of Light and Color in the Open Air," Dover Publications (1954).

Millie explained.

"There are times of quickening,
when everything's a jumble or a hologram
or both, when everything's as obvious
as the truth that nothing is, as the mystery
of sanity."

More often than it isn't, knowledge is discomforting,
and the dusty rooftop above a ravaged landscape
wasn't the Sheridarp Purphor had been hoping for.

"Can we go back? This place is too fast
and far too sharp. I prefer the slow and familiar:
fashionably accessorized currawongs,
pedestrians with magnolias for heads,
even warm Solarians. The everyday world."

"No problemo, we ascended to the rooftop
along a time-like trajectory—it's only the day
after tomorrow—and we'll return the same way."

But Purphor's plaintive complaining had
an unintended side-effect: it had called out
to the emptiness.

He heard a sound, the buzz of circular saws
in a carpentry shop, of a hundred transformers
with loose laminations, and he looked up
to see a swirling pixelated cloud:
a swarm of wasps, in the shape of a wasp—
the grotesque gigawasp.

"That's only a megawasp."

Millie had read his terrified mind.

"For a gigawasp, you'd need a cloud of megawasps."

Purphor paid scant attention,
because the cloud was drawing nearer.

Rooftop Facetime

Imperturbable Millie ignored the fearsome megawasp.

"I'm thinking that your so-called Sheridarp
is just a symbol, merely naming
what your soggy heart is seeking,
what you fear and crave,
and have never found."

He considered his reply.
Should he comment on the penguins,
recently arrived, conjecturing
that they were tourists visiting Sheridarp?

Some had cameras round their necks,
and their penguin guide
held a brightly colored flag
clasped in her beak.

Or perhaps he'd keep his counsel.
Scout wasps from the mother cloud
were buzzing all around them,
and an open mouth might prove to be
a strategical mistake.

Before he could decide, a dysmorphic shape
appeared above the parapet. It alighted
on the rooftop and sidled over
for a tête-à-tête with Millie.

The creature was a contradictory miasma,

animate and not, perilously dull,
a silhouette reminiscent of an enigma,
a straw hat hanging with a fur-lined
overcoat in a disused wardrobe.

He knew at once. It was a Dark Solarian.

Without a word of greeting,
the creature held its arms outstretched,
and points of coruscating light glowed
in Millie's aura. It was as if they'd always
been there, but only now were visible.

The creature drew her brightness to itself,
and as it did, Millie shed more light,
a radiant continuum peaking
at 380 nanometers,[3] streaming
to the Dark Solarian.

It was draining Millie's life force,
the fire of her anima.

~/~

The penguins cowered in the rooftop corners,
but Purphor cowered only slightly.

His plan was simple:
he'd distract the Dark Solarian,
offer up his own life force,
and Millie would survive.

Mother penguins would tell their chicks
his story, passed down through
the penguin generations, hopefully embellished,

---

3. One of the penguins had a spectrometer.

and without a mention of his missing hair.

The Personal Time Stream

In his penultimate moments, Purphor decided
to reveal his inner life.

"You're the one who make me nervous, Millie,
you're not as librarian as you appear,
and I'd like a latte."

"For now, please keep the penguins company.
There'll be time enough for refreshments
earlier in the time stream."

Millie thought for a moment, "Although, admittedly,
our personal moments are timed by the pulsing
of our hearts."

Her life force was a shower of refractive light,
dewdrops on a shattered windscreen,
a glister, a precipitate in the air.

She addressed the Dark Solarian.

"Poor parasite you are, always seeking life
you can't possess. After nightfall,
what you cannot hold is lost
into the lunar realm. You've drained
enough of me, it's time for you to go."

But the creature came even closer,
and the flux of Millie's fluid light intensified.

~/~

She threw her arms around the Dark Solarian.

"Is that close enough?"

A blinding flare of Millie's animatric energy
enveloped the sorry creature. It tried to pull away,
to disengage, but it was several lines too late.

Physics, Sheridarp-style

Matter and antimatter, in their uncomfortable alliance,
mostly text each other; minds and anti-minds,
over and beneath, may never touch; and parasitic
anti-dreams may never meld with the other kind.

Millie's being, her dream of luminiferous living,
had no place for dreary dead-end parasites.

As she held it, its anti-thoughts were annihilated:
the Dark Solarian imploded in blossoming ultraviolets.

~/~

Purphor fumbled in his pockets
for his dime-store sunnies,
but only found a ping-pong ball.

When the afterimages had faded,
and he could see again, he saw Millie,
slightly flushed. She'd drawn the energy
back to herself, and the Dark Solarian
was a pile of dust, or else the rooftop
needed sweeping.

"I work for her," he told the nearest penguin,
who was wearing welding goggles.[4]

---

4. Another penguin worked as a welder.

SHERIDARP

They auto-darkened when Millie
raised her arms and sent a fireball
of energy, superfluous to requirements,
shooting upward.

It burned the mega-cloud of wasps
to a shower of cinders, the remnants
of a million insects that were surely
guilty of something.

Coda

Millie has defeated the Dark Solarian
and the megawasp, and there is nothing more
to say.

~/~

From the rooftop, down and down
the silent page they went.

Purphor heard the hisses of an elsewhere night,
shoreward waves derailed from their sea tracks
to crash against graffitied cliffs, and occupy
the solitude between his thoughts.

Café Communicatrix

<the café économique has no fundamental
nature, it was sieved from the air of Sheridarp>

<a colorless canary flying far and low,
i chased my life but didn't catch it>

<don't try to hide, solarian fanboy, i see you
staring at her moiré fringes, her spectral
interference pattern>

<attend the pigeons, my little waifs, they fly
in tight formation from one treat to the next>

<first instincts wound us, our springs uncoil;
the wrong questions, inedible and indelible,
must still be asked>

~/~

I sighed, and lazy cinders wafted from my lips.

"It was a tale of the future, of longings,
re-weavings of our personal helioscopes."

But Millie knew my secrets.

"There's no need to explicatorialize.
You didn't write it, it's ghost-written."

I coughed up a little ash, examined
my translucent fingertips, and tried again.

"It was a reverse reverie,
a reinvention of reminiscences."

Buzzing silver bees were orbiting her
in tight ellipses, collecting
or returning something.

"Contextual truth is no one's forte,
but do they matter, the winding pathways
to an intersection? It's coffee break,
and the light of the golden penguin
is shining down on us."

A pigeon carried off my cinnamon toast.

About the Author

Steve Simpson lives in Sydney, and he's never been able to work out exactly what he does, although he would probably feed the cat if he had one. His poetry and short stories have appeared in various magazines and anthologies, and in the visual arts, works created with his image evolution software have been shown at several exhibitions. In the sciences, he's published over 200 research papers, most recently in clinical neurology, where he's developed a unique system for visualising mental states via EEG. Awards include the Peter Doherty Innovation Prize, for technology to make vehicles safer.